THE SCOTLAND YARD FILES

THE
SCOTLAND YARD FILES

MILESTONES IN CRIME DETECTION

Alan Moss & Keith Skinner

the national archives

First published in 2006 by
The National Archives
Kew, Richmond
Surrey, TW9 4DU
UK
www.nationalarchives.gov.uk

The National Archives was formed when the Public Record Office and Historical
Manuscripts Commission combined in April 2003.

Front jacket: street scene © Jack Carey /Alamy; police lamp © geogphotos/Alamy
Back jacket: telegram to Scotland Yard announcing PC Guttteridge's murder;
see Chapter 9 (MEPO 3/1631).

Jacket designed by Briony Chappell
Printed by MPG Books, Bodmin, Cornwall

Contents

Foreword

This is a book which gives many insights into how crime has been dealt with throughout the life of the Metropolitan Police. As well as telling the dramatic stories of a series of crimes which gripped the public's fears and imaginations at the time, the book recounts the advances that the police have made in their methods of securing evidence, improving detective skills and developing the technology now routinely involved in major crime investigations.

It is interesting to reflect on the fact that for the first 12 years of its existence, the Metropolitan Police had no detective branch. There has never been a period when so much emphasis has so exclusively been placed on police officers on the beat; but in 2006, we are once again trying to regain some of that continuity of street patrolling by introducing Safer Neighbourhood Schemes, with 3,500 staff exclusively dedicated to this task.

Sometimes the detail with which officers on the beat observed people's movements, as in the Daniel Good case, were remarkable; today, TV cameras try to achieve the same effect. The advancement of fingerprint technology and forensic science, particularly DNA, has transformed the detective's work, and one cannot help regretting that those nineteenth-century detectives did not have the scientific support with which their modern-day counterparts would probably have solved so many Victorian investigations.

In many ways this is a book which explains how Scotland Yard gained its world-wide reputation. Some of the detectives, as in the Road Hill House and the Hanratty cases, suffered personal criticism initially and I always savour the occasions when later developments have vindicated their actions.

I am immensely proud to lead an organization which has such a long track record of investigating crime effectively and protecting the public from dangerous criminals. I hope you will enjoy reading this book and share my sense of gratitude for the achievements of the detectives of Scotland Yard.

Ian Blair QPM MA
COMMISSIONER OF POLICE
OF THE METROPOLIS
NEW SCOTLAND YARD

May 2006

Preface

This book is largely about how Scotland Yard's detective officers achieved breakthroughs in crime investigation techniques, and how they dealt with incidents that have come to be seen as milestones in the history of Scotland Yard. Many of the stories that appear on the following pages are famous cases, and all of them caused a public stir at the time, but what were the *real* facts?

The public imagination was excited by the newspapers and by books written about some of the cases. But information in the public domain is not always true. Sometimes the witnesses' stories that appear in newspapers have been distorted by creative sub-editing, even when the complete truth was told to the journalist. Occasionally those who most wish to tell their story to the press are the least reliable witnesses. And famous cases generate gossip, misunderstanding and rumours, all of which can gather pace faster than the truth.

Detectives often keep back information from the public for the very understandable reason that they sometimes need to know whether a particular fact given to them has arisen from the witness's own experience rather than from knowledge in the public domain. Sometimes there is a legal reason for the police not to divulge some information about a case before it reaches court.

So for all these reasons, if we wish to find out the facts about these famous incidents, what better place can we turn to than the original files on which this book has been based?

When dealing with Scotland Yard, historians have the advantage that the Metropolitan Police Service (MPS), alone amongst British police forces, has been subject to the Public Records Acts, and the MPS therefore lodged its files at the National Archives. These have, subject to the Freedom of Information Act 2000, become available for public view. We hope that we can illustrate some of the rich treasures of the National Archives by our references to these original documents. Sometimes we have illustrated parts of the files; on other occasions the contents of reports or statements have simply been quoted. The *Case notes* section provides additional information for those interested in more details of files relating to each case and gives a short title for the files as well as the document reference in an attempt to be user-friendly for those interested in reading further.

We have aimed to improve access to some wonderful primary sources which, as well as being authentic, often help us to appreciate the pressure and emotions that must have been felt by those redoubtable detectives composing their accounts of traumatic events so many years ago.

Alan Moss & Keith Skinner
March 2006

Introduction: crime in the capital

The Metropolitan Police was established in 1829. Before this, the growing problem of crime and disorder had become a burning issue because there was no efficient way of enforcing the law and keeping public order. One of the worst cases of disorder was the Gordon Riots, which occurred in 1780 when Lord George Gordon led protests about Parliament's proposed extension of rights to Catholics. The Riots lasted four days, during which time many buildings, particularly those belonging to known Catholics, were destroyed and even Newgate prison was set on fire. There was no organization strong enough to deal with this situation. The magistrates, who were responsible for keeping order, were often far from resolute in fulfilling their duties, and the army, when it was called in, was not sufficiently agile to deal effectively with sporadic and fast-moving seats of disorder.

London was a city beset by poverty; in the 18th century, it was estimated that one in eight houses sold gin, a state of affairs well illustrated by William Hogarth's engraving *Gin Lane,* 1751. London had become a lawless place, and people of note, such as the prime minister, had to travel with an armed escort. The capital had no police force recognizable by today's standards.

There was one organization that did operate with some efficiency against crime; it was headed by the Bow Street magistrates, who, particularly under the leadership of Henry and Sir John Fielding, had established a system of regular, uniformed foot and horse patrols, and an experienced team of plain clothes officers, known as 'Runners'. These officers would investigate and arrest offenders when cases were brought to the magistrates' attention. However, Bow Street's impact on the general level of crime was limited and the patrols could never hope to cope with rioters. Their own court house was itself badly damaged during the Gordon Riots.

Sir Robert Peel, who became Home Secretary in 1822, had been Chief Secretary for Ireland from 1812 to 1818 and had set up the Peace Preservation Force there with a firm remit to deal with public order on a virtually paramilitary basis. His plans for policing London took on a different form, based on maintaining a continuous police presence on the streets. Colonel Rowan, who had been selected by Peel as one of the new force's first joint Commissioners, had served in the Peninsular War and knew about the military Shorncliffe system of small communicating scout patrols. He adapted it to become the basis of the beat system in which a constable patrolled a small area of streets following a regular pattern. The beats were timed so that there was always a policeman within a 15-minute walk from any point in the city. It was very different from keeping police officers in barracks until they were specifically called out in squadrons, as though they were an army.

Richard Mayne was the other joint Commissioner. As an Irish lawyer, he brought legal expertise to his role and served as Commissioner until his death, 40 years later in 1869. John Wray was appointed as the first Receiver for the Metropolitan Police District to deal with finance, equipment and buildings. Together they set about establishing their headquarters and police stations, recruiting officers of various ranks, and planning how the new police would carry out their duties.

The headquarters were established at Whitehall Place, but the public entrance of the premises was in Great Scotland Yard. It was not long before Scotland Yard became synonymous with the Metropolitan Police. When, in 1890, they moved into a larger building, designed by the famous architect Norman Shaw (see plate 2), the new headquarters was called New Scotland Yard, the same name as the present headquarters in Broadway SW1.

ROBERT PEEL'S INSTRUCTIONS

Peel's original instructions establishing the staffing and pay of the new Force survive at the National Archives:

> And I have now the satisfaction to signify to you my approval of your arrangements, and to sanction your commencing the New System of Police, with such an Establishment and Force as you have proposed viz:
>
> *Office Establishment*
> Commissioner's Clerks
>   One Chief Clerk
>   One Second Clerk
>   One Third Clerk
>
> Receiver's Office
>   One Chief Clerk
>   One Second Clerk
>
> *Police Force*
> 8 Superintendents
> 20 Inspectors
> 88 Serjeants
> 895 Constables
>
> I have also taken into consideration the amount of salaries to be paid to the Clerks for the Office, and the Salaries and Rates of Pay of the Police Force, and I have determined to establish the following scales.
>
> *Office Establishment*
> Commissioner's Clerks:
> Chief Clerk – A yearly Salary of £200, with an Increase of £10 for every year's Service in that Rank, until the Salary amounts to £400.
>
> Second Clerk – A yearly Salary of £150 with an Increase of £8 for every year's Service in that Rank, until the Salary amounts to £270.
>
> Third Clerk – A yearly Salary of £90 with a similar annual Increase of £5, until the Salary amounts to £150.

For the purpose of avoiding fractions in the Salaries of the Clerks, the year of Service is to be calculated in every instance from the Quarter day next after the date of the Letter from this office signifying the Clerk's appointment, unless the appointment bears a date on a Quarter day.

Receiver's Office
Chief Clerk. A yearly Salary of £200.
Second Clerk. A yearly Salary of £150.

Police Force
Superintendents – A yearly Salary of £200 each.
Inspectors – A yearly Salary of £100 each.
Serjeants – A daily pay of three shillings and six pence each [18p]
Police Constables – A daily pay of three shillings each [15p]

The pay of the Serjeants and Constables will be subject to certain deductions, which may be hereafter determined.   MEPO 2/10768

In September 1829, the first constables of the Metropolitan Police took up their patrols on the streets of the capital. By June 1830, the new force comprised 3,314 men allocated to 17 Divisions, each of which had a designated letter (A–H, K–V) and a Superintendent in charge.

ORGANIZING THE NEW FORCE

The first months of the new Metropolitan Police were taken up with the problems of organizing the new force and trying to develop public confidence in what was turning out to be a very effective, but more expensive, system of policing the streets of London. One of the most difficult problems for the Commissioners was maintaining discipline. It was a great change for members of the new force to adapt to the responsibilities of the self-discipline required for constables patrolling alone and capable of exercising legal powers of arrest on their own account. In the army they had been subject to constant scrutiny from ever-present non-commissioned officers and had been deployed in platoons or larger units. On the London streets they were often out of sight of their sergeants and inspectors. The scale of the discipline problem can be seen from the early records. These showed that in the first six months, 3,247 officers were recruited and allocated warrant numbers. Of that first band of pioneers, just over half (1,644) were dismissed, the most frequent cause being drunkenness:

Wt No	Name		Joined	Division			Date
1	William	ATKINSON	21/9/1829	C	Dismissed	Drunk for duty	29/9/1829
2	William	ALCOCK	21/9/1829	B	Dismissed	Drunk for duty	30/9/1829
3	William	ASHDOWN	21/9/1829	B	Dismissed	Absent from his beat	16/10/1829
4	Edwin	ALLEN	21/9/1829	B	Dismissed	Absent from his beat	17/10/1829
5	Edward	ALLEN	21/9/1829	B	Dismissed	Insubordination	20/10/1829
6	John	ANGELL	21/9/1829	B	Dismissed	Going into public house on duty	7/11/1829
7	John	ALLEN	21/9/1829	B	Dismissed	Going into public house on duty	15/11/1829
8	Thomas	ALDERSON	21/9/1829	B	Dismissed	Drunkenness	17/11/1829

MEPO 4/31

The first Instruction Book carefully set out the primary objects of the new Force and its organization. The police were to concentrate on *preventing* crime. This was also an echo from Rowan's Peninsular War experience where he had learnt, under Sir John Moore, that the quality of a regiment's discipline could be judged by the *absence* of floggings and other punishments taking place. Similarly, the *absence* of crime would be the mark of police effectiveness. Rewards and promotions would be linked to crime reduction, a forerunner of the modern performance-related pay system:

> The following General Instructions for the different ranks of the Police Force are not to be understood as containing rules of conduct applicable to every variety of circumstances that may occur in the performance of their duty; something must necessarily be left to the intelligence and discretion of individuals; and according to the degree in which they shew themselves possessed of these qualities, and to their zeal, activity, and judgement, on all occasions, will be their claims to future promotion and reward.
>
> It should be understood, at the outset, that the principal object to be attained is *'the Prevention of Crime'*.
>
> To this great end, every effort of the Police is to be directed. The security of persons and property, the preservation of public tranquillity

and all the other objects of a Police Establishment will thus be better effected than by the detection and punishment of the offender, after he has succeeded in committing the crime. This should constantly be kept in mind by every member of the Police Force as the guide for his own conduct. Officers and Police Constables should endeavour to distinguish themselves by such vigilance and activity as may render it extremely difficult for any one to commit a crime within that portion of the town under their charge.

When in any Division offences are frequently committed, there must be reason to suspect that the Police is not in that Division properly conducted. The absence of crime will be considered the best proof of the complete efficiency of the Police. In Divisions where this security and good order have been effected, the Officers and men belonging to it may feel assured that such good conduct will be noticed by rewards and promotion.   MEPO 8/1

There were no instructions for how to investigate a crime when the suspect had left the scene, nor was there any mention of detectives. The question of employing specialist detectives was not a matter that had simply been overlooked amid all the activity of setting uniformed officers to patrol their beats effectively; there had been a positive decision not to employ officers out of uniform at all.

Employing police officers in plain clothes attracted widespread public apprehension about loss of traditional civil liberties. In a spirited debate on the issue, many people expressed their mistrust about police officers secretly acting as 'spies', and there was a considerable body of opinion that distrusted the whole idea of civil liberties being put at risk by an organized police force, let alone one that employed officers who could not be instantly identified by their uniform. The question was settled in favour of members of the new force wearing a uniform at all times, even when off duty (see plate 3). It took some time to appreciate the distinction of employing officers in plain clothes to investigate crime more effectively as a detective branch.

The origins of 'Scotland Yard'

Scotland Yard is famous throughout the world as the name synonymous with London's Metropolitan Police Criminal Investigation Department (CID), but what were the origins of the name of the street from which the public entered the first Metropolitan Police headquarters?

In the 12th century, the land may originally have been given by the Saxon King Edgar to King Kenneth III of Scotland, where he built a residence for his annual journey 'to do homage for his kingdom of Scotland'. This was later used by other Scottish kings when they came to do homage, as barons of the realm, for the counties of Cumberland, Huntingdon and other English lands held by them. Sixteenth-century maps (see plate 1) refer to Scotland Yard to the north of Whitehall Palace, which had originally been built by Cardinal Wolsey. The Palace of Scotland was allowed to fall into decay by Henry VIII. It is believed by some that the last person to have lived at the palace was Margaret Tudor, sister of Henry VIII, who resided there after the death of her husband, James IV of Scotland, at the battle of Flodden Field.

Another theory is that the church of St Mary Rouncival once stood in the area. The Prior claimed a nearby farm possessed by a man named Adam Scott, and later the will of the then owner, Cecilie Kelly, bequeathed to her daughter 'the land known as Scottes Ground'. This could have been translated into 'Scottes Land' and then shortened to 'Scotland'. Alternatively, an old English word *scotte* meant rent and this could feasibly have referred to this area as being available for rent at one time, or where boat owners paid their fees.

Early in the 17th century, noted architects Inigo Jones and Christopher Wren lived in a house on the site. The poet John Milton also lived there during the Commonwealth of England under Oliver Cromwell's rule from 1649 to 1651. In later years, the land became divided into Great, Middle and Little Scotland Yards, of which only Great Scotland Yard exists today.

CHAPTER ONE

The first detective branch: Scotland Yard's early cases

In the first days of the Metropolitan Police, there was so much emphasis on preventing crime by putting police officers on the beat that there was no provision for detective officers at all. This was partly because the Bow Street officers still undertook an investigative role. When serious crimes were reported to the Metropolitan Police, it was the officer on the beat who dealt with the case until a more senior officer took over.

EARLY MURDERS

In the first 12 years of the new force's existence, some interesting cases were investigated under this system. One case, in 1831, involved the robbing of graves in order to provide bodies for medical training. At the time this was not a specific offence if no property had been stolen with the body, but the murder of an Italian boy by grave robbers in 1831 went beyond the activities of normal 'resurrectionists'. Their desire to find a fresh body that could be offered for sale to a medical school actually led them to commit a murder for this purpose. The case was investigated by local Superintendent Joseph Thomas of F (Covent Garden) Division, and resulted in the execution of John Bishop and Thomas Williams, amid much publicity and scandal.

Another difficult case involved the gruesome murder of Hannah Brown, whose torso was found in Edgware Road in December 1836. Her head was found 10 days later in a canal near Stepney, and her legs were found in

Camberwell. It was 10 weeks before the victim was identified by her brother, but in a tribute to diligent local detective work undertaken by Inspector George Feltham and PC Pegler of T Division, James Greenacre, who had been due to marry Hannah Brown, was successfully caught and convicted of her murder.

After these successes, there followed a series of unsolved murders that became the subject of a press campaign about the ability of the police to solve murder inquiries. The criticism of these five cases was sometimes unfair and there was no equivalent to the modern Press Bureau at Scotland Yard to give out more accurate facts to the public. The result was a gradual shift of opinion that led to the formation of a detective department.

In days before the opening hours of public houses became restricted, 21-year-old barmaid Eliza Davis was found murdered at the King's Arms public house near Regents Park, early on the morning of 9 May 1837. Her throat had been cut. Mr Wadley, the publican, gave the description of a customer who was in the habit of coming into the premises at about 6am. The murder investigation by Inspector Aggs was inconclusive, despite the help of PC Pegler, who had helped track down James Greenacre, and although a great number of possible suspects were traced, none was identified by Mr Wadley.

Another throat-cutting case involved the death of a good-looking 28-year-old prostitute, Eliza Grimwood, who seemed to have made her living by crossing over the Thames from Lambeth to meet men at the West End theatres. Inspector Field from L Division traced a cab driver who had brought Eliza and a gentleman back to her lodgings, and made numerous other inquiries, including, at one point, arresting William Hubbard, the dead woman's partner. Despite these heroic efforts, however, there was never sufficient evidence to close the case.

In June 1839, there was a fire in a watchmaker's shop in Soho and in one of the smoke-filled rooms, the police found the murdered body of the watchmaker, Robert Westwood. Over 80 of Mr Westwood's valuable watches had been stolen. There was no shortage of people who had a grievance against the prickly Mr Westwood, but whilst Superintendent Thomas Baker of C Division and Inspector Beresford traced many people who could help the inquest, there was no evidence to prove a case against any one suspect. Inspector Nicholas Pearce and Sergeant Charles Otway from A Division were drafted in to help the inquiry, and made many efforts to trace one of Westwood's neighbours, a paper-hanger by name of Nicholas Carron, who had fled to America immediately after the murder. But again the case remained unsolved.

The prospect of a reward helped to solve the fourth case, in which John Templeman of Pocock's Fields, Islington, was found murdered on 17 March 1840. A suspect pot boy, Richard Gould, was prosecuted, but the case failed for lack of evidence. After Gould's acquittal of murder, Sergeant Charles Otway pursued him to the ship in which he was about to sail for Sydney, armed with a warrant for the *burglary* of Mr Templeman's house, with which Gould had *not* previously been charged. Otway tricked Gould into signing a confession to the murder and brought him back to London, where Gould was then sentenced to transportation. Despite making the best of an unsatisfactory outcome from Otway's point of view, the inducement of a reward was held to be unfair, and Charles Otway's career as a potential detective came to an end. This did not hold him back permanently, however, because he retired in May 1853 as the Superintendent of C Division.

THE MURDER OF LORD WILLIAM RUSSELL

In May 1840, when Lord William Russell became the fifth murder victim, the newspapers had begun to expect failure in murder investigations, and the absence of an immediate arrest started to tip the scales of the argument towards appointing specialist detectives. The two uniform police constables who attended the scene near Park Lane, Mayfair, were followed by Inspector Tedman and a sergeant of the neighbouring D Division. Later Inspector Beresford and Superintendent Baker from C Division arrived (both had earlier been involved in the Robert Westwood case), and finally the Commissioner Richard Mayne himself attended the scene. This was not a case of an unknown victim, but a well-known member of the aristocracy and uncle to Lord John Russell, the Foreign Secretary. Even Queen Victoria took a personal interest in the case. The police were under pressure.

Richard Mayne, who regularly undertook personal supervision of contentious murder cases, called in the officer whom he judged best qualified for dealing with the case – Inspector Nicholas Pearce. He worked on A Division, which operated from Great Scotland Yard itself and often acted as a reserve of well-qualified officers to deal with special assignments. Pearce, who had joined the new force as a sergeant, had previous police experience, having been a Bow Street patrol officer. Pearce commenced his investigation by undertaking a careful search of Lord Russell's home, and soon found evidence implicating his manservant Courvoisier, who was later duly convicted and sentenced to death. The case was solved.

Nevertheless, only two days after the murder occurred, *The Times* published a leading article criticizing the detective ability of the new police. Despite the partial success of the Gould case, *The Times* asserted that Lord Russell's death was the fifth unsolved murder in recent years, and went on to praise the Bow Street officers:

> At the close of the second day after the commission of a barbarous murder in the house of a nobleman in a respectable and populous part of London, it appears that the police are without any clue that can lead to the discovery and apprehension of the murderer... During no previous period of the modern history of London have five cruel murders been committed within two years without some of the perpetrators having been brought to justice. We feel convinced that it is not from any absence of abhorrence at the crime; that it is not from any desire to screen or aid the escape of the offenders, that justice has been defeated, but merely from the inadequacy of the means employed to discover the guilty parties. In stating this opinion it must not be considered that we are disposed to blame the metropolitan police. On the contrary, from its first formation we have always approved of the system, and maintained that the public have derived great benefit from its operation. It is, however, impossible not to perceive that the excellence of the metropolitan police consists chiefly in the general protection it affords to the community, and in its prevention of crime by the constant display of its power and vigilance. The semi-military nature of the regulations by which it is governed, the duties required of its members in continually patrolling their respective

districts, render it almost incapable of engaging in such inquiries as can alone lead to the discovery of offenders. Whatever may have been the defects that formerly existed in our police establishments, the officers employed had acquired great experience, and were in every respect qualified for the duties intrusted to them. Neither their numbers nor their organisation were calculated to prevent crime, but as a detective police they seldom failed, and we are satisfied that to insure the apprehension of offenders recourse must again be had to their services...

The Times, 8 May 1840

Three weeks later, after Lord Russell's murderer had successfully been committed for trial at the Old Bailey, a letter appeared in *The Times* from 'Detector' responding to the earlier article and calling for the setting up of a plain-clothes detective force.

Sir, I observed with much pleasure, in the leading article of your excellent journal a few days back, some most able, judicious and temperate remarks upon the efficiency of the metropolitan police as a preventive force, and upon its total and unequivocal failure as a detective police; the last proposition having been so clearly, but unfortunately too truly, demonstrated by the recent dreadful murders and extensive robberies which still remain undiscovered...

I would suggest that 25 or 30 of the officers of the metropolitan police be selected with the greatest care and attention as to their activity, talent and integrity, to form a detective force only, and that it would be advisable that to this body some few of the most active, able, and respectable of the unemployed police-officers should be added, who might by their great skill and local knowledge render most important information and assistance. This detective force should, of course, be under the immediate control and direction of the Secretary of State and the Commissioners of Police. They should not wear a uniform unless it was thought necessary for them to do so upon State occasions or Royal processions...

The Times, 30 May 1840

Public opinion was starting to turn.

THE CASE OF DANIEL GOOD

Less than a year later, PC William Gardner of V Division (Wandsworth) was to find himself at the centre of a case that demonstrated the inefficiency of local Divisions attempting to undertake a London-wide inquiry and settled the issue for ever.

When PC Gardner was patrolling Wandsworth High Street on 6 April 1842, he was called to a shop because a pair of trousers had been stolen. A shop boy had seen the theft committed by Daniel Good (see plate 5), who was a resident coachman in Mr Shiel's household at Granard House, Putney Park Lane. PC Gardner, with two shop boys, went to the house and questioned Good. The officer then started a thorough search of the stables where Good worked and had almost finished when he decided to take a closer look at what he thought was a plucked goose. Bringing his lantern nearer, PC Gardner discovered that this 'plucked goose' was in fact part of a dead body. Before the officer could do anything, Good had run off, locking Gardner, the two shop boys, the estate factor and Good's own son inside the stable.

It took the party some time to escape from the stable, and the hapless PC Gardner called for assistance. Superintendent Thomas Bicknell arrived with Inspector Busain and later made out a report of his inquiries:

About 11pm on Wednesday 6th Inst. I received information that the body of a woman had been found in the stables of G Shiel Esq, Putney Park Lane, Putney...

During the search in the stables I questioned Houghton the gardener relative to Good's relations. He stated that they were not known and Good was so disliked that no one would associate with him... I immediately sent Constables in every direction to trace Good, who was known to many of the Police in the neighbourhood.... During the progress of the search, a portion of the bones (pronounced by the surgeon to be those of a human being) were found burnt in the fire place in the harness room adjacent to the stable, supposed to belong to the members of the murdered woman. I caused the coachman's boxes to be searched but did not discover any thing that could assist in tracing him. I ... directed the Inspector to lock the harness room and take away the key. MEPO 3/15

The brief details gleaned that first Wednesday night by Superintendent Bicknell were circulated from Wandsworth police station, and the public were alerted by means of 1,000 Wanted posters printed the next day. An additional method of circulating details of wanted criminals was by means of the *Police Gazette*, where Good's description appeared in the edition of 11 April 1842.

Back at Wandsworth, local Inspector Busain was also very busy on the case. He helped with searching the harness room in the stable block, and tried to identify the murdered woman. He took care of various exhibits, such as a blood-stained axe, and organized searches on Wandsworth Common, Wimbledon Common and Putney Heath looking for further clues. He even had to put a stop to the local parochial constable displaying the murdered woman's remains to the public on the following Sunday.

However, it was Sergeant Golding, the local Divisional officer, who made the best attempt to locate Daniel Good. He interviewed the staff and Daniel Good's 11-year-old son on the morning following the murder, and started to unravel Good's complicated private life. Good was an Irishman, about 46 years of age, with a 'wife' Jane Jones, also known as Jane Sparks, who took in washing in South Street, near Manchester Square, Marylebone. She looked after Good's son from an earlier attachment, and had visited Good some

---

The *Police Gazette*

This publication (see plate 4), which was sent to magistrates throughout the country, was published by Bow Street court, and had been started by the blind magistrate, Sir John Fielding, under the title *Weekly or Extraordinary Pursuit*. It was the first document that listed crimes, stolen property, and criminals against whom warrants had been issued. In 1786, under Sir Sampson Wright, later a Chief Magistrate at Bow Street, it was expanded, improved upon, and given the title *The Weekly Hue and Cry*. Later, in 1828, the publication became the *Police Gazette, or Hue and Cry*, shortened to *Police Gazette* by the time of the hunt for Daniel Good. It was only at the beginning of 1883 that Scotland Yard assumed responsibility for the publication, in a revised format and with photographs of wanted criminals.

days earlier at Putney, perhaps to challenge him about a new woman in his life. It seemed that Good must have killed her and then tried to burn her remains in the harness room. Good had indeed been 'courting' a 16-year-old girl called Susan Butcher, and he had been returning from visiting her at Deptford when the original theft of trousers had taken place. The police first thought that the body in the Putney stable might have been that of Miss Butcher, but this misunderstanding did not reduce the urgency of catching Good himself.

Sergeant Golding discovered Jane Good's address from the lad at 9.30am, and then went to 18 South Street but found, too late, that Good had already left there four hours earlier. Golding went to another address that Good might have used, leaving the local police to trace a cab driver who had picked up Good from Manchester Square. In a wonderful example of the detailed observations made by police officers on their beats, a night duty officer had made a note of the number of a cab that had been waiting outside Jane Good's address. The D Division police were therefore able to trace the driver and found that he had taken Good to Whitcomb Street, near Trafalgar Square. Cab drivers invariably returned to their local ranks after each journey so that their horses could be cared for, so it was not long before Good's next journey was discovered. He had taken another cab from Whitcomb Street to the Spotted Dog public house in the Strand.

Unfortunately, Daniel Good had slipped from the grasp of the pursuing police officers. It might have turned out differently if Good's son had been interviewed the previous evening about his stepmother's home. The lapse of time that occurred before any police officer went to South Street became a contentious issue.

The information about Daniel Good's escape was circulated internally within the Metropolitan Police by a system of route papers. Before the use of telephones or other electronic communications systems, officers met up with colleagues from adjoining Divisions at set times to exchange documents, and in this way copies were passed around the whole of London. The timing of the exchanges was duly recorded, and in fact a period of under five hours to alert the whole of the Metropolitan Police was not bad progress for its time. The route had reached B Division at 1.30am, A Division at 2am, F at

2.40am, E at 3.05am and so on, with each Division copying the information, giving it to officers on the beat and allocating men to undertake inquiries to trace the fugitive.

Manchester Square was on D Division and it fell to Inspector Tedman, the same officer who had attended Lord Russell's murder, to make a critical mistake in the Good case. He received the route at 3am, sent it on to S Division at 3.15am, but only read it to the D Division men arriving for duty at 6am. He and other officers knew Good, but only by sight. By 6am, Good had left 18 South Street and had already reached the Spotted Dog public house in the Strand (on F Division). Had the D Division officers, who had seen Good's cab at South Street, known about the murder, they might have been able to make an arrest. Inspector Tedman's decision to delay reading out Good's details to his patrolling constables resulted in his being suspended from duty for nearly six weeks without pay.

After the inquest hearing on the Friday, Inspector Busain and Sergeant Golding left Wandsworth and went to the Spotted Dog to brief Inspector Pearce, who had once again been called in by Richard Mayne to solve a difficult case. Pearce had just returned from investigating a murder in Eskdaleside, Yorkshire, and was assisted by Sergeant Stephen Thornton, rather than the disgraced Sergeant Otway.

Pearce went to the address of the fugitive's former wife, Molly (or Mary) Good, at 4 Flower and Dean Street, Spitalfields, but found that Good had moved on from there. The two officers did find Richard Gamble, who had earlier assisted Daniel Good to pawn some of his victim's property, and they also found clothing belonging to the murdered Jane Jones, but Daniel Good himself had moved on ahead of them. In fact, Good left London completely on Saturday 9 April.

Although Pearce had been appointed to conduct the investigation, this had not stopped officers from different Divisions enthusiastically duplicating inquiries. Pearce complained to the Commissioner in writing about a divisional sergeant whose inquiries at Molly Good's address were conducted so indiscreetly that Good might have become alerted.

Letters poured in from members of the public with various alleged sightings of Good, and suggestions about where he might be, and Pearce continued to pursue numerous lines of inquiry. However, in the end it was Thomas Rose, a former Wandsworth policeman who had known Good, who broke the case. Rose recognized Good while he was working on the new railway line at Tonbridge in Kent, and he was duly arrested. Despite the delay, Good was tried and executed at Newgate on 23 May 1842, some seven weeks or so after the incident. Molly Good and Richard Gamble were prosecuted for their part in helping Daniel Good while he was on the run.

Pearce's successful investigation in Eskdaleside was reported in *The Times*, but even this success and his appointment to pursue Daniel Good did not prevent the newspaper returning to attack the Metropolitan Police:

> The conduct of the metropolitan police in the present case, as in those of the unfortunate Eliza Grimwood, and Lord William Russell, and others, is marked with a looseness and want of decision which proves that unless a decided change is made in the present system, it is idle to expect that it can be an efficient detective police, and that the most desperate offender may escape with impunity. From the showing of the police themselves, it appears that at 9 o'clock on the Wednesday night they made a discovery of the murder, yet with the statement of the little boy (the son of Good) of his living at South-street, Manchester Square, they allowed the whole of the night to pass over without calling there; nor does it appear that they went there at all. Had they done so immediately, as they should have done, they would have found Good, as there is no doubt he slept there on Wednesday night, after escaping from the premises of his master, and at 5 o'clock on the following morning carried away the property he subsequently pawned and disposed of. This, however, was not all. On Friday, a sergeant of the D Division, No 14, having discovered the cab in which Good had been taken to the residence of his wife in Spitalfields, ordered the driver to take him to the same house, and on arriving there, in a conspicuous manner for such a neighbourhood, made no secret in telling Mrs Good he 'wanted' her husband for the murder of a female in Putney, and actually exhibited the large bill or placard describing the person of the supposed murderer. The circumstance soon got circulation through the neighbourhood, and thus the chances of detection were

considerably lessened, as there are unfortunately in that locality a class of persons who would do their utmost to protect an offender, no matter what the enormity of his crime might be, and prevent his being brought to justice.   *The Times*, 11 April 1842

The press criticism had its effect on the Commissioners and the Home Office. Concern in high places about the Daniel Good case had been followed by even more anxiety in relation to a second assassination attempt on Queen Victoria, on 29 May 1842, by John Francis. There was therefore much on the Commissioners' minds when, on 14 June 1842, Richard Mayne sent a special report to the Home Secretary, justifying the police action in relation to the Daniel Good inquiry and seeking an increase in the establishment of the Metropolitan Police for two inspectors and eight sergeants to act as detectives:

> The Commissioners feel themselves called on to bring this subject under the consideration of the Secretary of State, the occurrence of a recent case of Murder attended with circumstances of most shocking barbarity having caused much excitement in the public mind, the escape of the individual believed to be guilty upon the discovery of the crime and his remaining for a time undetected, being assumed to shew want of skill in the Metropolitan Police, and a defect of general organization applicable to detective duties.
>
> In the case now in question, the party charged (Daniel Good) having been apprehended and executed for the murder, the Commissioners will only observe that, according to the evidence, it seems clear:
>
> 1st ... that the Police were wholly without blame for not having prevented the crime...
>
> 2ndly The Commissioners do not consider any blame can reasonably be attached to the Constable for the escape of Good from the stable of Mr Sheill... The Police at Roehampton did not know of his cohabiting with a woman who lived in South Street, Manchester Square; nor had they any means of ascertaining these facts, or obtaining any information about him on that night.
>
> 3rdly With respect to Good's movements after quitting South Street, and his evading detection by the Police, the Commissioners find that

their general regulations for circulating the information in the first instance were not obeyed in the D and C Divisions of Police; and that if the usual and proper steps had been taken thereon in those Divisions, the party would most probably have been in custody within a few hours, and the Commissioners have for such neglect of their duty suspended the Inspectors of the C and D Divisions who were in fault after his first escape...

The official returns show that during the period (now nearly 13 years) since the Police have been established, 22 cases of murder have occurred. In these, 14 persons have been convicted, in seven others the guilty parties are, it is believed, known, but have escaped hitherto, either from having left the Kingdom, or from a want of sufficient legal evidence to obtain a conviction. As for instance in one of the cases (the murder of Mr Templeman) there is no reason to doubt that Gould, tho' acquitted, was the party who committed the murder; and he was afterwards convicted and sentenced to transportation for life for the burglary at Mr Templeman's at the same time that the murder took place. And in another case, the murder of a Police Constable (Culley) at the riotous meeting in Coldbath Fields in 1833, there is no reason whatever to doubt that the party who was tried but acquitted did commit the act...

The organisation of the Police was made in the first instance without any direct provision for the performance of such detective duties, as at that time the officers of Bow Street, the Magistrates' officers, and others, were considered exclusively applicable to this branch of Police. Amongst so numerous a body as the Metropolitan Police of course there will always be some possessing little of the zeal and skill requisite to discover and trace out a clue to the detection of a criminal. When the entire responsibility of the detection of criminals also was gradually cast upon the Police, arrangements were made ... for giving effect to the combined action of the whole Force for that purpose; at the same time ... one or more [officers] were specially charged with each case. For this special duty individuals more peculiarly qualified, from experience and superior intelligence, are selected in each Division. This employment of the men, however useful and necessary for the purpose, interferes with the regular

routine of duty assigned to each individual in the Police; and where the
inquiry is prolonged and requires the whole of his time to be devoted to
it, considerable inconvenience arises in supplying the place, and carrying
on the other duties, of the individuals so employed, and, in the case of
Inspectors and Serjeants, the interference with the other duties is still
more inconvenient...   HO 45/292

The Home Secretary's permission for the new branch was given on 20 June
1842, and, after a period of further planning and clarification, the new
detective force was announced in a memorandum of 15 August. A select
band of eight officers, including Nicholas Pearce, became the first official
detectives employed by the Metropolitan Police. The inspectors were paid
£200 and the sergeants £73 per year.

Nicholas Pearce's decision to transfer to the Metropolitan Police from
Bow Street was a fortunate one for the new force. He was later promoted to
Superintendent and was the first officer to take charge of a team of detectives at Scotland Yard. As time has progressed, the creation of specialist
detective squads has become routine for police forces, but in more modern
times those detectives have generally been drawn from the ranks of the
patrolling constables within the same overall total staffing level.

Pearce's career continued to flourish and he later became the Superintendent of F Division. By 1855, however, he had become worn out by
ill-health, and, in order to increase his pension by taking his service at Bow
Street into account, Sir Richard Mayne wrote a glowing testimonial about
him to the Home Secretary, Sir George Grey:

> ...by his great skill, experience and persevering zeal, [he has] succeeded
> in bringing many criminals to justice for most serious offences. Since his
> appointment to be Superintendent, he has also in several cases by his
> advice, and active co-operation, materially assisted in the detection of
> criminals; I have at all times found him ready to undertake duties for
> which he was so peculiarly qualified, in addition to the duties of his own
> office of Superintendent.   HO 45/6116

Nicholas Pearce was duly granted an annual pension of £166 that he drew for
three years until he died in Cornwall, on 15 December 1858.

CHAPTER TWO

Calling in the Yard:
reputations made at home and abroad

When places outside London had a serious crime to investigate, local people of influence turned to Bow Street for help, and for the first 10 years of the Metropolitan Police, it remained Bow Street to which the counties normally sent their requests for detective assistance. In April 1834, for instance, nearly five years after the Metropolitan Police had been formed, the magistrates of the village of Oare, Wiltshire, failed to make progress in tracing the person responsible for starting a serious fire in the village. Henry Goddard, a Bow Street officer, was sent down from London, and described in his memoirs how the magistrates 'came to the resolution laying the case before the Home Secretary, and asking for assistance to send down one of the Bow Street officers'. The local newspaper reported that Goddard arrived soon afterwards:

> About 12 o'clock on Sunday night last, a most destructive fire took place in the homestead of the Rev Mr Goodman, of Oare in this county, which consumed two large barns (one containing a rick of wheat just taken in) a cart house, two straw houses, a quantity of hay, a stable, waggons, carts etc; also 3 valuable horses, 24 pigs and a quantity of poultry, altogether amounting in value to nearly £1500... That the fire was wantonly caused, there is not the slightest doubt; the perpetrators of which must have been wretches sunk to the very lowest

> pitch of degradation, and governed by the most fiendish motives, as
> a more kind and benevolent gentleman than the Rev Mr Goodman
> does not exist. *Salisbury and Wiltshire Herald*, 26 April 1834

The following week, the newspaper was able to report on Goddard's success:

> Charles Kimmer, of Oare, near Pewsey in this county, hurdlemaker to
> Mr Ferris, at Draycott, has been committed to Fisherton gaol for trial,
> charged on his own confession with having on 20th of April, set fire to
> certain premises at Oare, the property of the Rev Maurice Hillier
> Goodman. Some strong evidence having been adduced against him, a
> Bow Street officer named Goddard apprehended him, and at once
> accused him of the crime, upon which he was so overwhelmed with
> the consciousness of his guilt, that he was determined to disclose the
> manner in which he had committed the rash act...
> *Salisbury and Wiltshire Herald,* 3 May 1834

Three years later, in February 1837, a 15-year-old boy named John Brill went
missing near Uxbridge. The boy had recently been a witness against poachers,
and a father of one of them joined the search party and found the boy's
murdered body suspiciously quickly. Mr Shepherd, the owner of the land,
lived close to both Bow Street and Scotland Yard, and asked Richard Mayne
to send an officer to assist Shackle, the Bow Street officer who was on the
case, and the local Uxbridge constables. The Commissioner duly obliged by
sending Sergeant Charles Otway of A Division. This was the first recorded
request for a Metropolitan Police officer to be sent to assist an investigation
outside the Metropolitan Police District, and was a reflection of the trust
placed in this officer before his detective career was halted by the problems
of the Richard Gould prosecution.

Three suspects were detained, but at the conclusion of the Coroner's
inquest, there was insufficient evidence to continue to hold them and they
were released. Two of the defendants, before being freed, wanted to see the
dead boy's body, still lying in an adjoining room. This was because of a
superstition that the blood of a murder victim would start to flow if it
were approached by the perpetrator of the crime. Whether they ever

1 Sixteenth-century map of Whitehall by Ralph Agas showing
the original location of Scotland Yard (MPEE 1/25).

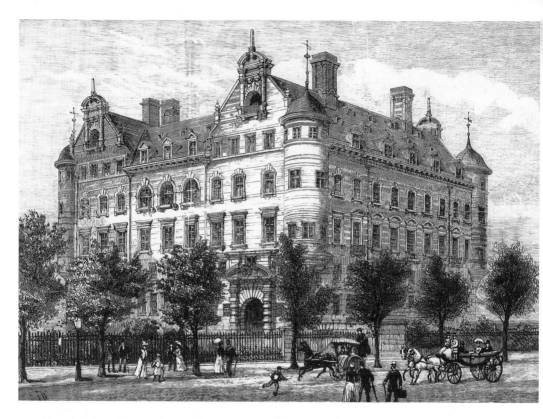

2 ABOVE The famous Norman Shaw building on Embankment originally intended as an opera house but then taken into use as New Scotland Yard in 1890.

3 RIGHT Original uniform of the Metropolitan Police 1829–64 including a top hat rather than a helmet.

4 OPPOSITE The *Police Gazette* originated in 1786 from Bow Street and was taken over by Scotland Yard in 1883. The edition of 11 May 1840 contained details of two important murders, those of Lord William Russell and John Templeman (HO 75/13).

POLICE GAZETTE.

Published by Authority.

CONTAINING

The substance of all Informations received in Cases of Felony and of Misdemeanors of an aggravated nature, and against Receivers of Stolen Goods, reputed Thieves, and Offenders escaped from Custody, with the time, the place, and the circumstances of the Offence. The Names of Persons charged with Offences, who are known but not in custody, and a Description of those who are not known, their Appearance, Dress, and other marks of identity. The Names of Accomplices and Accessories, with every particular which may lead to their Apprehension. A Description, as accurate as possible, of Property that has been Stolen, and a minute description of Stolen Horses, for the purpose of tracing and recovering them.

No. 175. MONDAY, MAY 11, 1840.

To Official Persons.—*By direction of the Secretary of State for the Home Department, the* POLICE GAZETTE *is supplied* GRATIS *to the undermentioned Officers:*

Mayors *or* **Chief Magistrates** *of Corporate Towns;*
Clerks *of* **Petty Sessions** *Divisions;*
Collectors *of* **Customs;**
Keepers *of* **Prisons;** *and the*
Chief Officers *of* **Police,** *in* GREAT BRITAIN *and* IRELAND:—*By whom it may respectively be obtained, on application to the* EDITOR,

MR. BURNABY, *Police Court, Bow-street, London, by letter,* PRE-PAID; *stating, if required by* POLICE OFFICERS, *the population of their Districts.*

Notice to the Public.—*Directions have been given by the Secretary of tate, that the Printer of the* POLICE GAZETTE *shal. be permitted to sell copies, at* ONE PENNY PER COPY. *They will likewise be forwarded* FREE, *oy Post, on the days of Publication (three times a-week), on condition of payment of the price in advance to the Printer, for not less than the succeeding* THREE MONTHS; *such payment to be continued so long as they shall be required to be sent.*

ALL APPLICATIONS *from persons desirous of receiving the* POLICE GAZETTE *under this Regulation, are requested to be addressed,* FREE OF POSTAGE, *to Messrs.* MILLS *and* SON, *Printers, Gough-square, Fleet-street, London.*

N.B.—*It is requested that all Communications for the purpose of obtaining, or giving, information respecting supposed offenders, or stolen property,* ESPECIALLY STOLEN HORSES, *may be addressed to the EDITOR.*

As no charge is made for the insertion of articles relating to stolen property in the POLICE GAZETTE, ALL *letters addressed to the Editor upon that subject* MUST BE PRE-PAID, *otherwise the required insertion will not be made; and letters transmitted in any other way than by the Post cannot be noticed.*

It is earnestly desired that persons sending informations to the Editor WILL BE PARTICULAR *in* SPELLING *the names of* PERSONS *and* PLACES *correctly; and in* WRITING *them* PLAINLY, *to prevent mistakes.*

INFORMATIONS.

MURDER AND MALICIOUSLY SHOOTING AND STABBING.

Whereas it hath been humbly represented unto the Queen that, on the night of Monday the 16th, or morning of Tuesday the 17th day of March, 1840, Mr. John Templeman, of Pocock's-fields, Islington, in the county of Middlesex, was barbarously Murdered at his residence, by some evil-disposed person or persons unknown; Her Majesty, for the better apprehending and bringing to justice the persons concerned in the Murder above-mentioned, is hereby pleased to promise Her most gracious Pardon to any one of them (except the person who actually committed the same) who shall discover his accomplice or accomplices therein, so that he, she or they may be apprehended and convicted thereof. And, as a further encouragement, a Reward of £200 is hereby offered by the Lords Commissioners of Her Majesty's Treasury, to any person (except as aforesaid) who shall discover the said offender or offenders, so that he, she or they may be apprehended and convicted of the said offence.—[*Bow-street.*]

Whereas it hath been humbly represented unto the Queen that, on the night of Tuesday the 5th, or morning of Wednesday the 6th day of May instant, the Right Honourable Lord William Russell, of No. 14, Norfolk street, Park-lane, in the county of Middlesex, was barbarously Murdered at his residence, by some evil-disposed person or persons unknown; Her Majesty, for the better apprehending and bringing to justice the persons concerned in the Murder before-mentioned, is hereby pleased to promise Her most gracious Pardon to any one of them (except the person who actually committed the same) who shall discover his accomplice or accomplices therein, so that he, she or they may be apprehended and convicted thereof. And, as a further encouragement, a Reward of £200 is hereby offered by the Lords Commissioners of Her Majesty's Treasury, and an additional Reward of £200 by the relatives of the deceased, to any person (except as aforesaid) who shall discover the said offender or offenders, so that he, she or they may be apprehended and convicted of the said offence.—[*Bow-street.*]

Escaped, from the Workhouse at Newton in Mackerfield, in the county of Lancaster, on Wednesday, the 6th instant, WILLIAM ATHERTON, commonly called CAPTAIN, being in custody on a charge of wilfully and maliciously Wounding Michael Conna, at Ashton in Mackerfield, in the same county, on the 4th of April last. Had on, when he escaped, a brown cap, round white fustian jacket, with waistcoat and trousers of the same material (the trousers patched at the left knee), blue striped linen shirt, black silk neckerchief usually tied in a sailor's knot, and quarter boots laced at the side. He stands 5 feet 8 inches high or less, is about 24 years of age, broad set, dark sunken eyes, small whiskers, hair and whiskers rather sandy-coloured, broad round face, light complexion, and has been employed as a turner in an iron-foundry.—Any person apprehending the said offender and lodging him in any of Her Majesty's Gaols, shall receive £5 Reward, on application to Ralph Hunt, constable, of Haydock; or to James Jones, deputy constable, Warrington.—[*Bow-street.*]

very red face, and dressed in black; the other about 20 years of age, 5 feet 6 inches high, and wore a brown frock coat and Albert stock. It is probable they left Nottingham about Saturday noon, by the Railway. The Cheque was indorsed by the elder, 'W.H. Wild.'—Whoever will give information to William Barnes, high constable and superintendent of police, Notingham, as shall lead to their apprehension and conviction, shall receive £5 Reward.—[*Bow-street.*]

ROBBERY FROM THE PERSON.

About 10 o'clock on the night of the 3rd instant, R. Hubbard was stopped in his gig, near the Halfpenny Tollbar, by Five Men, and robbed of a gold hunting Watch, 'No. 8024,' maker's name 'Barrett, Cornhill, London.'—Whoever will give information of the offenders, so that they may be brought to justice, shall, on conviction receive a Reward of £20.—Information to be given to B.H' Cheney, superintendent of police, Boston.—[*Bow-street.*]

HOUSE-BREAKING.

On the night of the 30th ultimo, the Premises of H. Kolle and Son, No. 1, North Mews, Little James-street, Gray's-inn-lane, were broken and entered, and the following property stolen therefrom, viz.: about 80 lbs. of Horse-hair, a part of them drafts; a Bag, supposed to be marked 'R 6,' containing 1 cwt. 2 qrs. 27 lbs. net of gathering Hair; about 1 cwt. of gathering Hair, sorted; also, 20 or 30 lbs. of Pickings and tangled Hair.—Any person giving such information to H. Kolle and Son, as will lead to the apprehension and conviction of the offender or offenders, shall receive a Reward of Twenty Pounds.—[*Bow-street.*]

Some time between the hours of 3 and 8 o'clock in the afternoon of Thursday, the 7th instant, during the absence of the family, the House of W. Finch, of Potscomb, Oxon, was entered by the cellar-window, and the following articles stolen therefrom, viz.: a blue straight Coat, single-breasted; a drab kerseymere Waistcoat, two pockets in each side; five Guineas, 7s. in fourpenny-pieces, about 3s. in copper, two Razors in a case, with the name 'Finch,' marked inside the case. Supposed by two Men, who were seen lurking about; one dressed in a short smock-frock, the other in a drab jacket, appearing like railroad men.—Whoever will give information of the offenders to Joseph Seymour, constable of Thame, Oxon, shall, on conviction, be handsomely rewarded.—[*Bow-street.*]

On the night of the 6th instant, or early the following morning, the Dwelling-house of Mr. Joseph Dobell, tailor, Headcorv, Kent, was broken and entered, and the following articles stolen therefrom: a yard and a half of black Cloth, and a piece about enough to make a waistcoat; about four yards of Oxford Mixture; about two yards and a half of Cantoon, and five yards of a narrow stripe; three yards of dark brown, three yards of light twilled, and about two yards and a half of speckled ditto; about eight yards of stout cotton Cord; about ten or twelve yards of an inferior dark small rib Cord. Also a large beaverteen Shooting jacket lined through

Some time in the night of the 1st instant, the Shop of Mr. William Furniss, draper, of Tarporley, was broken into and the following articles stolen therefrom, viz.: a quantity of black gauze Ribbon, figured and plain; a quantity of coloured silk Handkerchiefs; a quantity of black silk Handkerchiefs; a quantity of coloured Shawls, various sizes; a quantity of coloured gauze Shawls, various sizes, and a quantity of white cotton Shawls.—Whoever will give information of the offender or offenders shall, on conviction, be handsomely rewarded, on application to Edward Jones, police-officer, Tarporley, Cheshire.—[*Bow-street.*]

The House of the Rev. J. N. Goulty, in the Western road, Brighton, was broken into on the night of the 30th ult., and the following property stolen therefrom, viz: six table Forks, four Spoons, a Fish-slice, a Gravy-spoon, and ten Tea-spoons, all silver, and marked 'G.' in old English; three silver small Spoons, marked 'H.'; two silver small Spoons, marked 'W.'; four silver small Spoons, marked 'M. W.'; a silver sauce Ladle, marked 'G.' in old English; three silver Dessert-spoons, marked 'G.' in old English; a silver Dessert-spoon, marked 'W. N. G.'; a silver Dessert-spoon, marked 'Goulty'; three silver Salt-spoons, marked 'W.T.'; a silver pickle Fork with ivory handle; a plated soup Ladle, not marked, and a plated toast Rack, not marked.—Information to be given to H. Solomon, chief officer of police, Town-hall, Brighton.—[*Bow-street.*]

HORSE AND CATTLE STEALING.

On Tuesday, the 5th instant, about 6 o'clock in the morning, two young Men applied to Mr. Taylor, 'Golden Lion-inn,' Aston-street, Birmingham, for a Horse and Gig, stating their intention of proceeding to Coleshill and back that day, since which time neither of them have been heard of, and it is supposed they have stolen the same. The younger of the two is short and rather stout, dark eyes and hair, about 5 feet 5 inches high, scarcely any whiskers, and had on a Petersham coat; the other is a little taller and thinner, with bushy whiskers. The Horse is black, 5 years old, stands 15 or more hands high, switch tail, has not been docked, has been badly fired on the hind feet for ring-bones, is a good-looking blood horse, and goes a little lame at starting. The Harness is tolerably good, with quite a new collar. The Gig is painted dark green and black, lined with dark moreen cloth, has two new spring blocks painted once over with black, and a new extra plate on the off side spring.—Whoever will give such information as shall lead to the recovery of the Horse and Gig and conviction of the offenders, shall receive £10 Reward, on application to Mr. Taylor aforesaid.—[*Bow-street.*]

Stolen, on the night of the 7th instant, or early the following morning, from Church Over, in the county of Warwick, a Light Grey Mare, 4 years old, about 15 hands high, large head, with the hair knocked off two places on the forehead, pinched on the near shoulder, a piece of skin gone from the off hind leg below the hock, rough heels, switch tail, had on four new shoes, and has been burnt for the lampers.—£5 Reward will be paid to any person causing the apprehension and conviction of the offender or offenders and recovery of

5 RIGHT Court sketch of Daniel Good, whose escape from police played a part in the creation of the detective branch.

6 BELOW RIGHT Constance Kent, who confessed to the murder of her brother five years after the event, and OPPOSITE the prison licence documenting her release in July 1885 (PCOM 4/62).

7 BELOW LEFT Professor Alfred Swaine Taylor FRS (1806–80) of Guy's Hospital, a forensic toxicologist who launched the journal *Elements of Medical Jursiprudence* and helped to lay the foundations of forensic science.

To Sup with 7275 and then to Directors

ORDER of LICENCE to a CONVICT
made under the Statutes 16 and 17 Vict., c. 99, s. 9, and 27 and 28 Vict., c. 47, s. 4.

Day on which Convict is due for Discharge 18th July 1885

WHITEHALL, *19th* day of *July* 1885.

HER MAJESTY is graciously pleased to grant to *Constance Emilie Kent* who was

convicted of *Murder.*

at the *Assizes holden at Salisbury in and*

for the *County of Wilts*

on the *19th* day of *July 1865.*, and was then and there

sentenced to ~~be kept in Penal Servitude for the term of~~ *Death which sentence was afterwards commuted to Penal Servitude for Life*

and is now confined in the *Fulham* Convict Prison,

HER ROYAL LICENCE to be at large from the day of her Liberation under this Order, during the remaining portion of her said term of Penal Servitude, unless the said

Constance Emilie Kent shall,

before the expiration of the said term, be convicted of some indictable Offence within the United Kingdom, in which case such Licence will be immediately forfeited by Law, or unless it shall please Her Majesty sooner to revoke or alter such Licence.

This Licence is given subject to the Conditions endorsed upon the same, upon the breach of any of which it will be liable to be revoked, whether such breach is followed by a Conviction or not.

And Her Majesty hereby orders that the said

Constance Emilie Kent

be set at liberty within Thirty days from the date of this Order.

Given under my Hand and Seal,

49113
Constance Emilie Kent

LICENCE TO BE AT LARGE.

£200 REWARD

MURDER

Whereas HARRIET BUSWELL, aged 26, was found with her throat cut, at No. 12, Great Coram Street, Russell Square, on the 25th December, 1872.

The Murder is supposed to have been committed by a Man of the following description, who was seen in company with the Deceased on the evening of the 24th, and to leave the house at 7 a.m. on the 25th:—Age 25, Height 5 feet 9 inches, Complexion swarthy, red spots on face, Black Hair, no Whiskers or Moustache, but not shaved for two or three days, Stout Build; Dress, dark tight-fitting Coat, dark Billycock Hat, a Foreigner (supposed German).

TWO HUNDRED POUNDS REWARD

Will be paid by Her Majesty's Government to any person who shall give such Information and Evidence as shall lead to the discovery of the Murderer; and the Secretary of State for the Home Department will advise the grant of

Her Majesty's most Gracious Pardon

To any Accomplice not being the person who actually committed the Murder, who shall give such Evidence as shall lead to a like result.

Information to be given to SUPERINTENDENT THOMSON, Police Station, Bow Street, London, or at any of the Metropolitan Police Stations.

METROPOLITAN POLICE OFFICE,
4, Whitehall Place, London,
16th January, 1873.

E. Y. W. HENDERSON,

The Commissioner of Police of the Metropolis

HARRISON & SONS, PRINTERS IN ORDINARY TO HER MAJESTY, ST. MARTIN'S LANE.

10 LEFT Adolf Beck (top and bottom) was twice wrongly identified and convicted for frauds committed by William Weiss, alias John Smith (centre) (MEPO 3/154–5).

8 OPPOSITE ABOVE Reward notice seeking information in the search for the killer of Harriet Buswell on Christmas morning 1872 (MEPO 3/110).

9 OPPOSITE BELOW An identity parade as pictured in *The Graphic*, 1887.

11 BELOW Percy LeFroy Mapleton, as pictured in *The Daily Telegraph* of 1 July 1881, the first image of a wanted fugitive published in a British newspaper.

12 RIGHT Formal declaration of the execution of Percy LeFroy Mapleton signed by the Under Sheriff of Sussex (HO 144/83/A6404).

DECLARATION OF SHERIFF.
AND OTHERS.

31 *Vict. Cap.* 24.

We, the undersigned, hereby declare that Judgment of Death was this Day executed on Percy Lefroy Mapleton otherwise Arthur Lefroy } in Her Majesty's Prison of — at Lewes —— in our Presence.

Dated this 29th Day of November 1881

—— Under Sheriff of Sussex ——.

—— Justice of the Peace for Sussex ——

—— Governor of the said Prison.

—— Chaplain of the said Prison.

PRINTED AT HER MAJESTY'S CONVICT PRISON, MILLBANK. 2—80.

THE RAILWAY TRAGEDY.

SEARCH FOR LEFROY.

GOVERNMENT AND RAILWAY REWARDS.

We understand that the Government and the London, Brighton, and South Coast Railway Company have each offered £100 reward for information leading to the apprehension of the murderer of Mr. Gold. Yesterday the police continued their efforts in various directions, and two or three persons were apprehended in different places on account of supposed resemblance to Lefroy, but they were afterwards released. Late on Wednesday went the news abroad somewhere about Bexley that a man, closely resembling the supposed assassin of Mr. Gold, was tramping to Gravesend. An inspector of the Metropolitan Police tracked the man mile after mile for a long distance, but at length the officer seemed to have got off the scent. It was excusable, for the man had already been taken into custody on suspicion. He turned out to be a decayed gentleman who had the misfortune to resemble in gait and plausibility the supposed perpetrator of the railway tragedy. The face, however, was not the face of Lefroy, and the local police were not long in setting him at liberty, making amends by the hospitality of a good breakfast and the present of a shilling with which to pay his railway fare onwards. He did not, however, take to the train, but to the highway, and thus met the inspector who had originally started in search of him, and was re-arrested, only, however, to be again shortly afterwards set free. It would seem that a succession of reports reached the authorities from places on the route to Gravesend, and the police were led to make a vast number of needless and fruitless inquiries. It was stated in London yesterday afternoon that Lefroy had been taken at Greenwich, and afterwards with a great amount of certainty that he had been captured in a railway carriage between London and Windsor. There turned out to be not the slightest foundation for these statements. Meanwhile, the police and railway authorities are making a thorough search along the line, in the hope of finding some money, or the knife or revolver with which it is believed the crime was committed. Special attention is being directed to the spot where Mr. Gold's hat was found, as there is there a thick growth of underwood, where anything might easily lie concealed unless thorough search was made.

With regard to Mr. Gold's movements on the day of the murder it has been conclusively ascertained that he visited his shop in East-street, Walworth, and received from his manager £38 5s. 1d., and it has been further found that he banked this money. So far as has been at present discovered he did not draw the dividends on his wife's account. Inquiries have also been directed with a view to obtain information as to any possible connection of the suspected person with any of Mr. Gold's present or former servants. The investigation on this point has resulted in absolute information to the effect that Lefroy was not known to or by any of the servants employed by the deceased gentleman since he went to reside at Preston Park.

The collar found on the line, and supposed to belong to the murderer, whoever he may be, has been compared with those usually worn by Mr. Gold, with the result that they do not correspond. At Lefroy's lodgings no shirt collars

at Lefroy's residence shows house he behaved with com He went to his room, remove his head, washed himself clothes. Afterwards he e seeking his cousin's (M explained to her in a manner that he had was going to the d wounds dressed. He out at the back way, the utmost ease. A house by the police ea but beyond the bloo dence was found to with the crime. An house, but no othe cabman, whose evid of Müller, has been Wallington, possibly with a if his experience can lead to the criminal of the same stamp.

Subjoined we give a sketch portrait by a gentleman who knew Lefroy and had frequent opportunities of noting his characteristics. It has been attested as an excellent likeness by several persons with whom Lefroy came into close contact.

The police have issued the following further notice :

Murder.—Percy Lefroy Mapleton, whose apprehension is sought for murder on the Brighton Railway, left the Fever Hospital, at Islington, at 9.30 on the morning of Tuesday, June 28. Description : Age 22, middle height, very thin, sickly appearance, scratches on throat, wounds on head, probably clean shaved, low felt hat, black coat, teeth much discoloured. Information to the Director of Criminal Investigations, Great Scotland-yard, or at any police-station.

The attention of licensed victuallers, tobacconists, railway officials, stage carriage conductors, and cabmen is very particularly directed to this matter.

In the interests of justice it is well that the public should be fully informed in regard to Lefroy's personal appearance. The following particulars may be relied upon as accurate. He is very round-shouldered, and his whole overcoat hangs in awkward folds about his spare figure. His forehead and chin are both receding. He has a slight moustache, and very small dark whiskers. His jaw-bones are prominent, his cheeks sunken and sallow, and his teeth fully exposed when laughing. His upper lip is thin and drawn

to his assailant he had reckoned without was very active and powerful. A d struggle ensued, and, as the rough was not getting the best of it, he seized the money, and swore that if his fellow travellers did not give up their money he would run them through. The valet capitulated, delivering up not only his money, but a ring that he wore. The other, more resolute, got out of the carriage window with the intention of reaching the guard, securing himself firmly on the footboard, after many desperate attempts on the part of the scoundrel to throw him on the line. At this juncture the train was travelling at the rate of forty miles an hour. Scrambling along to the next compartment, our correspondent, letting the window down, found it occupied by an old lady, who screamed dreadfully when she saw him, the more so as she had heard the scuffle in the next compartment, and naturally enough thought he had been murdering somebody and now came to treat her in the same fashion. In this way he passed six compartments, letting down the windows as he reached them in order to secure a firmer hold. At the sixth compartment from the one he left the passengers invited him to come inside. He told them what had happened, but they hindered instead of helping his purpose, and detained him in the belief that he was a madman, the lady passengers meanwhile betraying the extreme terror they felt at the alarming intrusion. The train reached Blisworth at eleven o'clock, and when it stopped there was a pretty general demand that he should be arrested. As there were only the night porter and ticket collector at the station, it was resolved that none of the parties concerned should be allowed to leave the train, and a telegram was sent to Rugby to have a sufficient force to deal with the affair. At Rugby a cordon was formed round the carriages, and the gentleman to whom we are indebted for this narrative went to the carriage where he had originally been with the dread on his mind that the poor valet might be dead. The valet was bewildered and could say nothing. His troublesome fellow-traveller was arrested after a desperate struggle, and lodged in Rugby Police Station. The jewel case was restored to its owner, but the valet had to wait for the result of a subsequent trial to get back his money and ring. Ultimately the ill-intentioned ruffian was tried at Northampton, and sentenced to eighteen months' imprisonment. The porter, to whose obstinacy so much trouble was due, was severely reprimanded by the Court.

Another correspondent, a City solicitor, reminds us of a curious incident contemporaneous with the Müller outrage. He says : "I was in the habit of going home by rail at that time, and persuaded the local population of their innocence is not known. In those days the coroners and magistrates took over investigations from the police at a far earlier stage.

MURDER IN ESKDALESIDE

In March 1842, it was Scotland Yard alone which received the request to send a detective to the small Yorkshire township of Eskdaleside, about six miles from Whitby, to investigate a murder that had already appeared several months earlier in Bow Street's *Police Gazette,* with details of a £100 reward for information leading to the conviction of the offender.

On 14 September 1841, some farm workers found 61-year-old Jane Robinson murdered in her own home, while her husband had been out at Egton market. There was widespread shock at the brutality of the crime, especially as it had occurred in the late morning in broad daylight. The desk, from which 31 sovereigns had been stolen, bore the fingerprints of the culprit, and a bloody knife that had apparently been the murder weapon was found behind the kitchen fire.

After the arrest of a number of men who proved their innocence and were subsequently discharged, a surgeon gave his opinion that the victim must have met her death before 10 in the morning. This coincided with a visit to the farmhouse by the 48-year-old local miller, William Hill. He was sent to York to stand trial for the murder on 27 November 1841. At the trial, the jury heard from the farm workers who had seen William Hill ride past without speaking to them; from William Robinson, the victim's husband, who had been owed money for corn by Mr Hill, who paid off his debt soon after the murder; and from a servant, Mary Frankland, who had heard Mrs Robinson accuse the miller of cheating her out of eighteen pence. The case against him was weak, however, and Mr Hill was acquitted.

But Mr Hill had been unable to throw off the suspicions held about him by the local population. The case aroused the attention of Constantine Henry Phipps, the Marquess of Normanby, who, as Home Secretary from 1839 to 1841, would have been responsible for the Metropolitan Police. His country seat was at Mulgrave Castle, 10 miles from Eskdaleside, and he had attended some of the hearings of the Whitby magistrates dealing with the case. In March 1842, with the magistrates' agreement, the Marquess wrote not to Bow Street, whose officers had been abolished by then, but to Scotland Yard, thus creating a milestone in the history of the Metropolitan Police. A detective from Scotland Yard was sent to investigate a murder in the provinces. The officer chosen to perform this duty was none other than Inspector Nicholas Pearce.

Inspector Pearce soon concluded that William Hill had indeed been innocent. There had been signs of a man having hidden in a loft over a cow house, the roof of which had been broken to provide a hole for observing the farmhouse 20 yards away. He found that a man dressed in a white shooting jacket had been seen near a wood where a pocket book had been found, along with a loaf that had been baked outside the county. The servant Mary Frankland described a former farm employee, Thomas Redhead, whom she had seen in July the previous year. Redhead had borrowed half a crown from her, but had never appeared again, and his current address was unknown. Redhead's description matched the man seen near the wood, and Pearce therefore set about tracing him.

Pearce made a guess that Redhead had travelled from Stockton, and started making inquiries in that town and others, before learning that his quarry had died from smallpox on 4 January 1842 at Shildon, six miles outside Bishop Auckland, where Redhead had worked on the excavations for the Shildon railway tunnel. The 50-mile journey from Shildon to Eskdaleside could have been made by using the new railway line that passed by the farm.

Pearce established that his suspect had been penniless before the murder, but had been spending sovereigns immediately afterwards, mostly on a venture to open a grocery shop with Mr Tomlinson, who had comprehensively cheated his new partner. Redhead had sued Tomlinson in a court in Durham, but had been too frightened or inarticulate to proceed with the case, and had never been able to maintain a sense of pride afterwards. He had apparently been about to make some form of confession to his landlady before he died. Furthermore, Pearce found blood on Redhead's pocket book near to an entry made within a few days of the murder.

The Whitby magistrates agreed with Pearce's conclusions about Thomas

Redhead's guilt, and were highly complimentary of his efforts. The details of Pearce's investigation were reported in local newspapers and then in *The Times* of 11 April 1842, just at the time when Daniel Good was on the run and the Metropolitan Police were under pressure. Pearce provided an example of what could be achieved by an efficient detective, and the compliments paid to Pearce were in stark contrast to *The Times'* general criticism of the Metropolitan Police's ability to solve murders in London.

ROAD HILL HOUSE

One of the eight founding members of the detective branch was E Division's newly-promoted Sergeant Jonathan Whicher, who had joined the Force in September 1837. By 1860, five years after Pearce's retirement, he was the senior Detective Inspector in the branch. It was Whicher who was called in to investigate the cruel murder of a 3-year-old boy, Francis Savill Kent, at Road Hill House, in the village of Road, Wiltshire. But he did not receive the acclaim received by Pearce at Eskdaleside.

The case aroused enormous public interest, and revolved around the household of Samuel Kent, a 59-year-old factory inspector. Mr Kent had a large family and had married the children's governess, Mary Drewe Pratt, after his first wife died. One of his daughters from his first marriage, Constance Emily, was 16 at the time of the murder. His second wife had given birth to a daughter, Mary Amelia, in 1855, and to the ill-fated son, Francis Savill (known as Savill), in August 1856. By Saturday, 30 June 1860, when the tragedy was discovered, the second Mrs Kent was eight months pregnant with another child. The children's nurse, Elizabeth Gough, also lived in the house.

Savill was found to be missing from his cot at 7.15 on the Saturday morning. The house was searched but there was no trace of the child. One of the windows was partly open, but there was no other sign of potential illegal entry into the house. Mr Kent personally drove to Trowbridge to see Police Superintendent Foley of the Wiltshire police; he did not wish to rely on a messenger, or to spend any time speaking to the two constables whom he passed on his way.

It was not long before Savill's little body was found in an outside privy, with his throat cut and a stab wound in his chest. During a search for blood-stained clothing and other clues, one of Constance's nightdresses was found to be missing and was never recovered.

A controversial inquest took place, in which the coroner restricted proceedings by only calling as witnesses the servants of the house, police officers and medical practitioners. It needed the jury to insist that the family itself should be questioned. Even then, the coroner only questioned Constance and her 14-year-old brother William, and never examined Mr and Mrs Kent. Unsurprisingly, the inquest verdict was 'wilful murder against some person or persons unknown'. The jury were far from satisfied that all attempts had been made to identify the culprit. It was a horrific crime, and neither the police nor the local establishment had the wherewithal to deal with an investigation into such a traumatic incident in the house of a local man of substance.

There was no love lost between Mr Kent and the local villagers, many of whom might have relished the gossip of an affair between Mr Kent and the resident governess, Mary Pratt, long before the death of the first Mrs Kent. And it would not have taken much imagination for a curious local to have wondered whether the failure of the children's nurse, Elizabeth Gough, to have noticed the child being taken from her room might perhaps have been due to her sleeping in another bed.

The officer in charge of the investigation, Superintendent Foley, was under pressure to identify the culprit, but suffered from the authoritarian directions, or perhaps the deliberate interference, of Mr Kent, whose actions and statements were inconsistent at times. At one stage, the Trowbridge magistrates held Elizabeth Gough in custody, during which time she hinted at her suspicions about 16-year-old Constance, who was known to be head-strong and had run away from home on one occasion. The Trowbridge magistrates then decided to write to the Home Secretary, Sir George Cornwall Lewis, asking for the assistance of a detective officer from Scotland Yard.

Sir Richard Mayne wrote a letter turning down the request on the basis that the County Police had been established, and 'the assistance of London officers was now seldom resorted to'. It is not known whether the fact that the request had come direct from the magistrates, rather than with the agreement of the local police, had been a factor in Sir Richard Mayne's decision. However, a week or so later, the request to Scotland Yard from the magistrates was repeated, backed up by a separate request from Mr Kent's solicitors. This finally persuaded Sir Richard Mayne to send down Inspector Jonathan Whicher, who commenced work more than two weeks after the crime had been committed. He started by watching the hearings of the magistrates, who adjourned to Road Hill House to question Mr Kent, and then allowed Elizabeth Gough to go free.

Whicher concluded that the child's throat could not have been cut without loss of blood, and the likelihood of the perpetrator's clothing being blood-stained was therefore an obvious line of inquiry. Most of the household's night attire was eliminated from suspicion, but Whicher discovered that one of Constance's nightdresses was missing. The nightdress was supposedly lost in the washing being done by a local woman, but the Kents' housemaid had briefly been distracted by Constance while packing the laundry basket, and there had been an opportunity for Constance to have removed the garment, together with any incriminating blood stains on it. Whicher discussed his tentative conclusions with the magistrates, but instead of them giving him further time for investigations, they issued him with a warrant to arrest Constance, despite Whicher's reluctance to be seen to be diverging from the conclusions of the local police. Whicher's hand was forced. He wrote a report on 22 July 1860:

> I beg further to report, for the information of Sir Richard Mayne, in reference to the murder at Road, that on Friday last the Magistrates again met for the purpose of hearing the result of my enquiries as far as I had gone, and to take my opinion as to the best course for them to pursue.
>
> After due consideration of the evidence, I stated I should be able to lay before them, on a future occasion against Mr Kent's third daughter 'Constance' aged sixteen, viz. the fact of her Bed gown being missing, and the statement of two of her late school fellows ... which would shew the animus the prisoner had expressed to them towards the deceased in consequence of the Father and Stepmother shewing great

partiality towards him and the other two children by the second marriage; and other suspicious circumstances, for instance the fact of the murder taking place soon after she came home for her holidays, that she was the only person who slept alone except her Brother, also home for his holidays (and who, I have some suspicion, assisted in the murder but at present not sufficient evidence to apprehend him); the fact also that it was no doubt effected by some person who slept in the house, and that the person who committed it, did so in their night dress, and the circumstance of the body being found in the same privy in which she cast her female apparel … before absconding from her house, on the occasion referred to in my former report....

There was some doubt as to her physical capability to commit the act, but I find that she is a very powerful young girl, and I am informed by her school fellows that [whilst] romping she was dreaded by all the others, frequently displaying her strength of which she was in the habit of boasting, and as to her moral capacity she appears to possess a very strong mind...   MEPO 3/61

When Jonathan Whicher brought Constance to court, he asked the magistrates for an adjournment to enable him to search for further evidence, and the magistrates remanded her in custody to Devizes jail for a week. Whicher then sent a telegram to London for assistance, followed by a report to Sir Richard Mayne, by this time the sole Commissioner at Scotland Yard. Whichner asked for the assistance of either Richard Tanner or Adolphus Williamson, two sergeants who were both later to become distinguished detectives in their own right.

Whicher later expressed his thanks for the arrival of Sergeant Williamson, 'as I am very unpleasantly situated as regards acting with the County Police in consequence of the natural jealousy entertained in this matter by them, especially as our opinions differ, they suspecting Mr Kent and the Nurse; and should it appear in the end that my opinions are correct, they would be considered at fault, but I have studiously endeavoured to act in concert with them as far as possible.'

At the next court hearing, Mr Kent and his solicitor had instructed a barrister from Bristol to defend Constance. The local police, sceptical about the case against Constance Kent, were present in seniority and numbers. Jonathan Whicher must have felt isolated, especially as he had no lawyer to support the prosecution case. In the intervening period, he had not been able to find Constance's missing nightdress nor any further evidence against her. The barrister was able to dominate the court and to win most, if not all, of the exchanges that arose during the hearing, which resulted in Constance Kent being released on bail. There was not enough evidence to keep her in prison, but she had not yet been formally discharged.

Jonathan Whicher had applied his judgement, but had been forced into proceeding against Constance Kent purely on circumstantial evidence. Constance Kent's release led to Whicher becoming a scapegoat. The magistrates wrote to Sir Richard Mayne and to the Home Secretary supporting Whicher's actions, but many were critical, even in Parliament. The MP Sir George Bowyer intervened in a Parliamentary debate to declare:

> The recent investigation with regard to the Road murder afforded striking proof of the unfitness of some of the present officers. An inspector named Whicher was sent down to inquire into the matter. Upon the slightest possible grounds, merely because one of her nightgowns happened to be missing, that officer arrested a young lady who lived in the house where the murder was committed, and assured the magistrates that he would be prepared in a few days to produce evidence which would bring home the murder to her. *Hansard* vol. CLX, 15 August 1860, p.1340

The *Frome Times* of 8 August 1860 commented, 'With reference to the course pursued by "the Detective" we cannot refrain from observing, that if the conduct of Mr Whicher is a fair sample of their proceedings, it will be long before Detectives will be tolerated again in this part of the country...'

Regardless of the result of the court case against Constance Kent, the Wiltshire Police still retained responsibility for pursuing the case. They prosecuted Elizabeth Gough – and that case also ended in failure.

Constance Kent went to a finishing school in France and then returned to England, where she stayed at a religious institution in Brighton. After a period of five years, during which time she increasingly turned to religion, she had a serious talk with her Mother Superior, and, following that conversation, she journeyed to Bow Street magistrates court. The newspapers reported this dramatic turn of events:

> Yesterday afternoon Sir Thomas Henry, the chief magistrate of Bow Street, received information that Miss Constance Kent, formerly of Road-hill-house, near Frome, had arrived in London from Brighton for the purpose of surrendering herself to the officers of justice for the perpetration of the memorable crime [of the Road Hill Murder]...
>
> Shortly before 4 o'clock, Mr Superintendent Durkin and Mr Williamson, chief inspector of the Detective force, conducted their prisoner to the private room of Sir Thomas Henry... Sir Thomas Henry, addressing the prisoner, said 'Am I to understand, Miss Kent, that you have given yourself up of your own free act and will on this charge?'
>
> Miss Kent: 'Yes Sir.'
>
> Sir Thomas Henry : 'Anything you may say here will be written down, and may be used against you. Do you quite understand that?'
>
> Miss Kent : 'Yes Sir.'
>
> Sir Thomas Henry: 'Is this paper, now produced before me, in your handwriting and written of your own free will?'
>
> Miss Kent: 'It is, Sir.'
>
> Sir Thomas Henry: 'Then let the charge be entered in her own words.'
>
> The charge was then entered as follows: 'Constance Kent, of 2 Queen Square, Brighton, charged upon her own confession with having, alone and unaided, on the night of the 29th June 1860, murdered at Road-hill-house one Francis Saville Kent'...
>
> It is alleged that before making her confession Miss Kent had written to her father, announcing the decision which she had arrived at, with a view, it is supposed, of saving him the sudden shock of learning it first from the newspaper reports.   *The Times*, 26 April 1865

Constance Kent confessed to carrying out the murder alone and unaided. The case was solved. She was remanded to appear before the Wiltshire Assizes, pleaded guilty, and was sentenced to death, before being reprieved by Queen Victoria (see plate 6). Her confession did not answer all the questions that the people raised about the precise circumstances of what happened in Road Hill House that night in June 1860, but it did vindicate Jonathan Whicher's judgement. Whicher had retired in 1864, suffering from 'congestion of the brain', having been at the centre of this controversial case that illustrated the shortcomings of the system for investigating crime against local men of substance, the inexperience of some of the county police forces, the difficulty of collaborating, especially alone, with a provincial police force that had not itself made a request for assistance, and the workings of the inquest and magistrates' court systems of the day.

THE FIRST RAILWAY MURDER

Richard Tanner, whose assistance Jonathan Whicher had requested, was later promoted to inspector. Four years after the Road Hill House case, he was involved in an investigation that included a number of significant milestones: the first murder on a railway, the first pursuit of a fugitive across the Atlantic by ship, and one of the first extradition cases from America dealt with by Scotland Yard.

The story started on the evening of Saturday, 9 July 1864, when two bank clerks boarded a Highbury-bound North London Railway train at Hackney and found their first-class compartment to be soaked in blood. In the compartment was a walking stick that had apparently been used as a weapon, a leather bag belonging to a Mr Briggs, and a hat. There was no sign of a victim of any attack. Soon afterwards, the victim, Mr Thomas Briggs, Chief Clerk in the bank of Messrs Robarts, Curtis & Co in the City of London, was found unconscious on the railway track with a serious head wound. His hat and his pocket watch were missing, and he died the following evening. The murder had been carried out on the five-minute journey between Bow and Hackney Wick.

Richard Tanner was put on to the case. There were two immediate lines of inquiry. First, a description of Mr Briggs' stolen gold watch and chain was circulated. Information soon came in that a silversmith in Cheapside had taken in Mr Briggs' watch chain on the Monday, two days after the attack. The silversmith, who rejoiced in the name of John Death, described the man who brought it in as having a sallow complexion with thin features, wearing a black frock coat and vest, and probably German.

The second clue was that the suspect appeared to have put on Mr Briggs' hat by mistake and to have left his own hat behind at the scene of the crime. The suspect's hat was unusual; it had been cut down and was therefore shorter than Mr Briggs' silk top hat. The alteration had been made not by a hatter, but by somebody who also sewed neatly. A £300 reward was offered for the apprehension of the murderer, which resulted in a cab driver called Matthews coming forward. He had purchased a hat for a young German tailor called Franz Müller, who had given Matthews' young daughter a box with Mr Death's name on it on the Monday afternoon. Müller had given Mrs Matthews an address in Bethnal Green where he would be staying, but when Inspector Tanner called there, his suspect had already left England on the ship *Victoria* bound for America.

Tanner went to Bow Street, where an extradition warrant was signed by the Chief Magistrate. Then he set sail for New York from Liverpool in the faster steamship, *SS City of Manchester,* accompanied by Sergeant Clarke, the silversmith Mr Death, and the cab driver Jonathan Matthews.

The speed of the new steamships was illustrated by the fact that Tanner and his team reached New York no less than three weeks before the arrival of the *Victoria*, and there was considerable press excitement about the forth-coming confrontation. Despite fears that Müller would be alerted, Richard Tanner achieved total success, and was able to send a telegram to Scotland Yard: 'The *Victoria* has arrived at New York and Müller has been arrested. The hat and watch of Mr Briggs were found in his possession. Müller protested his innocence, and the legal proceedings in reference to his extradition are progressing.'

Extradition proceedings were, even then, likely to create political problems. Britain was not popular in America at the time, and there was sympathy for Müller from fellow Germans, so Müller's legal representatives could draw on political arguments, even if the evidence itself was clear-cut. Despite this, Commissioner Newton in New York authorized the extradition to Britain, and the party returned to London via Liverpool. Crowds waited at Euston station to express their indignation at Müller, who was driven off to Bow Street court, which until its closure scheduled for June 2006 has remained the traditional court for dealing with extradition cases. There were some suggestions that there had been another man in the carriage assisting Müller when he attacked Thomas Briggs, but it was Müller alone who was sent for trial at the Old Bailey. He was convicted and executed at Newgate in November 1864.

Mr Briggs' son was grateful for the way in which his father's murderer had been brought to justice, and offered a reward of £55 to Inspector Tanner 'as a small token of our appreciation of the courteousness and delicacy with which he conducted the case in all communications with the family.'

This was a case in which Richard Tanner started to build up Scotland Yard's international reputation. *The Times* said in October of that year that no murderer had excited such interest since Courvoisier for the killing of Lord William Russell in June 1840, or Dr William Palmer for the poisoning of Mr Cook in May 1856. The newspaper readers would have been aware that Dr Palmer had become notorious for poisoning a fellow race-goer in Rugeley, Staffordshire, and stealing his winnings. He had drawn to himself such public hostility that Parliament had passed an Act making it possible to transfer a trial to London if a defendant was unlikely to receive a fair trial in his own county.

The detection and successful prosecution of Franz Müller had satisfied the public that violence on the new railways would be efficiently dealt with. It also indicated the commitment that Scotland Yard showed in the first chase of a fugitive across the Atlantic, and provides an early example of using an extradition treaty to bring a criminal to justice.

CHAPTER THREE

Forensic science:
from bloodstains to DNA

A few months after Constance Kent's confession had vindicated Jonathan Whicher, Richard Tanner thought that he might be entering another cauldron of local politics and jealousy. He was sent, in 1866, to investigate another contentious case, this time in Duddlewick, near Bridgnorth in Shropshire. An 18-year-old orphan, Edward Edwards, had been found murdered at a water mill where he had lived with his uncle, John Meredith, since the age of seven when his parents had died. The local police had arrested one suspect, James Childs, who had blood-stained clothing, but he had been discharged by the court because of lack of evidence against him.

THE DUDDLEWICK MURDER

The request for help came to Scotland Yard in January 1866 in the form of a letter from Lieutenant Colonel Edward Cureton, who at the time had been the Chief Constable of Shropshire for a little under 15 months. The request was therefore directly from the Shropshire force, and in agreement with the local magistrates. The force had been formed in 1840, under the direction of Captain Dawson Mayne, Sir Richard's younger brother. Regardless of whether or not Sir Richard had a soft spot for the Shropshire force, it was becoming clear that detective expertise from London was regularly in demand, even though police forces had been established throughout

England. The smaller forces were often short of the experience required to deal with difficult investigations, and the practice of calling in Scotland Yard was to continue for at least another 100 years.

Scotland Yard sent in Inspector Tanner, who was careful to be seen to be *assisting* the local Superintendent, Mr McWilliam. It was not long before Tanner suspected the victim's uncle, John Meredith, of having struck his nephew down in a fit of temper, but, in his report of 25 January to Sir Richard Mayne, he found himself 'thwarted by the local Coroner who was friends with vital witnesses'.

The victim was a poor boy with no property worth stealing, and Tanner found no reports of strangers in the area. His interviews with the household revealed that John Meredith had told his sister Mary that he had been to the mill after breakfast, but could find no trace of the boy. Then Meredith had gone to church without expressing any anxiety about his nephew, who was late for presenting his accounts for inspection. On his return from church, he procrastinated further by eating a meal and smoking his pipe for an hour. Then, with a neighbour, he searched other areas before finally going to the mill, where the key was found in its normal place, over the door. Edward Edwards was found severely injured in the mill and was

---

An early merger: Bridgnorth Police Force

Bridgnorth was an early example of controversy caused by plans to amalgamate police forces in the name of efficiency. In June 1853, magistrate Sir Baldwin Leighton told a Parliamentary Committee how Bridgnorth (the nearest town to Duddlewick) had recently attempted to amalgamate its police force with Shropshire. Both sides agreed to this and Bridgnorth then requested that its one constable (the entire strength of its force) should join the county police. The mayor of Bridgnorth and one of the county magistrates met to discuss the situation, but when it was clear that the policeman could not read, the mayor asked for the agreement to amalgamate to be set aside out of loyalty to his local man. Eventually the merger did take place, but not until six months later when the constable had been found another job in Bridgnorth.

carried to the house, but died shortly afterwards. Some of John Meredith's clothing was blood-stained and he appeared to have tried to wipe off some of those stains.

Richard Tanner reported his findings to the magistrates who issued a warrant and remanded John Meredith in custody. Tanner then returned to London, knowing that the Chief Constable and the magistrates considered the prisoner to be guilty, and were taking the responsibility for prosecuting him despite the fact that the evidence was circumstantial.

Meredith's blood-stained clothing was taken down to London by Shropshire's Sergeant Cox, where it was examined by one of the very first forensic science experts, Professor Alfred Swaine Taylor of Guy's Hospital (see plate 7). Professor Taylor's report of 31 January 1866 provides an early example of the analysis of blood stains:

> On Thursday January 25th 1866, I received ... certain articles of clothing for a microscopical and chemical examination. These articles were; 1 An overcoat of dark speckled woollen, much worn; 2 A shirt, and 3 A pair of trousers of grey woollen.
>
> *1 The Overcoat*
>
> This was dirty and much stained ... On examination ... showed that they were not caused by blood.
>
> *2 The Shirt*
>
> This was soiled as from ordinary wear. On the left sleeve at from four to eight inches above the waistband, there were four small spots having the usual appearance of fresh blood dried in the fibres of the stuff. They were small, round and about one-eighth of an inch in diameter. They were distinct but near together, two and two, one being a lengthened spot as if by sprinkling ... They had the usual character of blood which had dropped in a liquid state on the stuff, and in drying, had coagulated within the fibres. They had the same shade of colour, and had probably all been produced at the same time. They were plainly visible, and no attempt had been made to remove them or wash them out...
>
> It is impossible to fix with any certainty the date at which these spots were produced on the shirt. After three or four days, blood spots on

calico or linen undergo but little change of appearance. When I first examined them with a view to form an opinion of date (January 25th) they appeared to me to be comparatively speaking fresh, and they may have been produced at any time within three or four weeks previously to that date.

3 The Trousers

They are of grey woollen; they presented in the front, chiefly about the flap and in the upper part of the legs, numerous superficial stains of a pale red colour. Portions of these were cut out and submitted to microscopical and chemical examination. The result is that these stains have been caused by blood falling or dropping on the front of the trousers, and from their appearance, I infer that while wet they have been superficially wiped or sponged. Small clots of blood may still be seen by the microscope buried in the fibres of the woollen and closely adhering to them, but these do not appear on the surface of the trousers. The wetting must have been slight, i.e. on the surface of the cloth, for in no instance have these stains produced corresponding marks or stains on the calico lining of the trousers...

Conclusions

The conclusions which I draw from this examination and analysis are:

1 The stains on the overcoat have not been produced by blood.

2 The small spots or stains on the left sleeve and the flap of the shirt have been caused by blood and are comparatively recent.

3 The pale red coloured stains on the front of the trousers have been caused by blood apparently removed while wet by a wet cloth or sponge. These have the appearance of fresh or recent blood.

4 The stains or spots found on the lining of the flap of the trousers and in the lining of the left pocket have been caused by blood, but they are apparently of old date.   MEPO 3/80

At the magistrates' court, John Meredith claimed that the blood stains on his clothes must have occurred when he helped to carry his fatally wounded nephew to his bedroom. Unfortunately Professor Taylor was not in court to give his opinion about whether Meredith's explanation was likely or not.

A forensics pioneer: Professor Alfred Swaine Taylor (1806–80)

Professor Taylor (see plate 7) was appointed as Professor of Chemistry and Medical Jurisprudence at Guy's hospital in 1834, and, two years later, published the first of many editions of the journal *Elements of Medical Jurisprudence*. Superintendent Cuthbert, the first superintendent to have served at the Metropolitan Police Forensic Science laboratory, credited this journal with laying the foundations of modern forensic medicine. Taylor was a forensic toxicologist and gave expert medical evidence in court in poisoning and other cases. He is also known as one of the 'fathers of photography' for developing the use of hyposulphate of lime as a fixing element.

John Meredith was a churchwarden, and his status in the town was demonstrated by the applause from the public gallery when he was acquitted on 9 February. The coroner, unknowingly agreeing with Tanner's first fears, said 'It is quite a Road murder'; he concluded his inquest six weeks later without affecting the outcome of the case. However, he did ensure that he heard the personal evidence of Professor Taylor, who was reported in the *Shrewsbury Free Press* of 24 March 1866 as telling the inquest jury that 'the blood of animals is so much like human blood that you cannot distinguish between them'. The science of analysing blood (serology) had not yet been born, and the expertise in analysing blood splashes had not been developed.

DEVELOPMENTS IN BLOOD ANALYSIS

Thirty-five years later, in 1901, the *preciptin* test was developed from rabbit-based serums by Paul Uhlenhuth and Jules Bordet; its purpose was to indicate whether or not blood was human. The test was first used in that year to investigate a child murder in Germany, and formed part of the evidence that disproved the claim of a suspect, Ludwig Tessnow, that stains on his clothing were of wood dye.

Early in the twentieth century, Karl Landsteiner started to discover blood groups (e.g. A, B, O). Then, during the First World War, doctors found that it was dangerous to give patients the wrong type of blood transfusions.

In 1925, scientists realized that blood groups could be determined from some people's body secretions, such as saliva and urine, and in March 1932, the conviction of an ex-police officer, Maurice Freedman, for the murder of a London typist, Annette Friedson, was notable for the evidence of Dr E. Roche Lynch. He testified that blood of the same group as the murder victim's was found on Freedman's razor. The blood group was relatively rare – it was found in only 3% of the population – and this evidence helped to secure Freedman's conviction.

By the mid-1960s, the work of Drs Margaret Pereira and Brian Culliford at Scotland Yard's forensic science laboratory on analysing blood reached a point where they could link the identity of a suspect with a blood stain to a very high degree of accuracy. More factors within blood were being discovered, and the analysis of protein within human blood sometimes led to the creation of additional sub-groups and rarity factors.

THE MURDER OF CLAIRE JOSEPHS

A murder case in 1968 illustrates what could be achieved at that time. On 7 February 1968, Bernard Josephs returned home to Shortlands, Kent, to find his wife Claire lying dead in their bedroom. There was no sign of any forced entry to the flat, but a partly-made soufflé, a cup of coffee, and some biscuits on a plate suggested that Mrs Josephs had been interrupted from cooking to receive an unexpected visitor. The police started to interview anybody who might have visited the flat, and in due course came across Roger Payne, the husband of one of Mrs Joseph's friends. He had scratch marks on his hands and a bruise on his forehead, which he attributed to an accident while repairing his car that had broken down that evening and had caused him to arrive home late in Maidstone.

Scotland Yard's forensic science laboratory was asked to examine some blood-stained clothing, in much the same way as Professor Taylor had been commissioned over 100 years previously. The scientists also examined some items found in the flat, as well as Payne's Morris 1100 motor car. Dr Margaret Pereira described the various blood samples in her statement, and proved the link between Payne's car and the unusual blood group of the murdered woman. Her statement, made available by courtesy of the Metropolitan

Police Service, proved that a handkerchief found at the scene was stained with both the victim's and Payne's blood groups:

NMR 16 SAMPLE OF BLOOD LABELLED 'CLAIRE JOSEPHS'
This was of Group AB,MN,PGM2–1. This combination of blood groups is found in approximately 0.6% of the population of this country

PW9 SAMPLE OF BLOOD LABELLED 'ROGER JOHN PAYNE'
This was of group A,M,PGM2–1. This combination of blood groups is found in 4.4% of the population of this country...

NMR 23 BLOOD-STAINED HANDKERCHIEF
This was a man's white handkerchief. Blood stains of group AB,MN (Claire Joseph's group) and of Group A,M (Payne's group) were found on this handkerchief...

PW10 MORRIS 1100 CAR FPE 937 B
[...] Inside the pocket on the same door there was a little fairly heavy blood staining in the lower corner towards the back end. This was human blood of Group AB,PGM2–1 (Claire Joseph's group). This group combination is found in approximately 1.2% of the population of this country. MN grouping was not possible.   MEPO 2/11137

Detective Superintendent John Cummings, who was in charge of the inquiry, reported some of the other scientific evidence that would be so notable in this case. The murder victim had been wearing a cerise dress, made of very distinctive and unusual fibres, which were an exact match with residue found on Payne's hat, coat and jacket.

As well as having an unusual blood group, Claire Joseph's distinctive dress fibres had been transferred to Payne's clothing. In the hundred years since Professor Taylor's report on the Duddlewick Mill exhibits, forensic science had made remarkable strides in the examination of blood-stained and other clothing. The series of links, taken together, made a compelling case for connecting Roger Payne to the scene of the murder. He was convicted and sentenced to life imprisonment on 24 May 1968 at the Old Bailey.

By 1974, some samples could be shown to have a 1 in 10,000 chance that a blood stain did not belong to a given suspect. In 1983, the murder of three members of the Laitner family near Sheffield was solved by a forensic science laboratory team who found a blood stain that could only arise, on average, once in 50,000 people. The laboratory had already analysed such a rare sample from a local criminal called Arthur Hutchinson, and he therefore became the prime suspect. His palm print was also found at the scene. Hutchinson was later convicted of the crime.

DNA TESTING

These scientific advances were eventually superseded by the use of DNA (deoxyribonucleic acid), a more fundamental part of living tissue that carries the genetic information of each individual human being (and other animals). It provides a unique 'signature' for each person, based on heredity, and can therefore identify people with absolute certainty from samples taken from flesh, bone, hair roots and body secretions, such as sweat. It is only identical twins who share the same DNA, but their fingerprints will be different.

The structure of DNA was discovered by scientists Jim Watson and Francis Crick in Cambridge in 1953, but it was in September 1984 that Dr Alec Jeffreys and his team at Leicester University, who were researching gene evolution and heredity in illness, looked at the complex patterns in X-ray films of their tests, which appeared like bar codes, and suddenly realized that they had found a method of recording details of biological identification. Alec Jeffreys, later knighted for his work, collaborated with Dr David Werrett and Dr Peter Gill of the Forensic Science Service to demonstrate that it was possible to extract DNA from old crime scene stains, and these techniques then superseded blood grouping for crime scene investigation purposes.

In Spring 1985, DNA was used to resolve a deportation dispute by proving that a boy was a full member of a family based in Britain, and some months later, the first paternity dispute was determined. Appropriately enough, it was a local Leicester case in which, on 21 November 1986, DNA evidence first decided a criminal case. Ironically, it secured the acquittal of Richard Buckland, a young man who had been wrongly charged with murder.

THE MURDERS OF LYNDA MANN AND DAWN ASHWORTH

The case involved the two apparently linked murders of 15-year-old Lynda Mann from Narborough in 1983, and Dawn Ashworth, also 15, from nearby Enderby in 1986. A month after Dawn Ashworth's death, the police became aware that Richard Buckland, a 17-year-old kitchen porter from Narborough, had been in the vicinity at the time of Dawn Ashworth's death, and he became the prime suspect. Detective Superintendent Painter's report, made available by courtesy of Leicestershire Constabulary, included the details of Buckland's interviews with police:

> 18. On 8th August 1986, BUCKLAND was arrested at his home address on suspicion of the murder ... BUCKLAND admitted that he had stopped his motor cycle and had accompanied the girl ASHWORTH part of the way along Ten Pound Lane.
>
> 19. ... During these interviews, BUCKLAND gave numerous accounts of what had happened whilst he was with the girl, retracted his various accounts, some in total, others in part, then reiterated some facts. During the evening of that day, BUCKLAND made admissions to the officers of facts which clearly indicated a knowledge of what had happened far beyond imagination [and] which were consistent with facts obtained during the enquiry. When questioned over these matters, he admitted he was responsible for ASHWORTH's death, that his admissions were the truth and he did not retract any of this account.
>
> 20. Later that evening samples were obtained from BUCKLAND by the witness Dr SMEETON...

Unsurprisingly, Richard Buckland was charged with Dawn Ashworth's murder and was remanded in custody while the full prosecution case was prepared against him. His blood samples were then submitted so that a forensic science analysis could confirm or disprove his confession. The analysis would also provide the same means of checking whether he was responsible for the earlier linked murder of Lynda Mann.

As expected, the forensic scientists found a common DNA link with each crime scene, and could thereby prove that the same man had been involved. Much more dramatic, however, was the fact that DNA also showed that the double murderer was *not* Richard Buckland. After three months in prison, his confession was confirmed as being unreliable, and he was released by Leicester magistrates. DNA had been used in a criminal case for the first time, and it had established innocence rather than guilt. A later report, dated 27 October 1987, by Detective Inspector Thomas, explained what then happened:

> ...On 19th November 1986, the murder incident room was re-opened in the light of the information from the Forensic Scientist which showed that the semen at both scenes had the same 'genetic fingerprint'.
>
> 32   In order to eliminate large numbers of people resident in the villages of Narborough, Enderby and Littlethorpe from the murder enquiry, male residents in those areas between the ages of 13 years and 33 years were requested to supply, on a purely voluntary basis, blood and saliva samples to be tested against samples recovered at the scenes of both murders. The sampling commenced on 5th January 1987 and, up until 19th September 1987, 4,583 persons had supplied the samples requested...

The police undertook a massive operation to track down the man who possessed the DNA genetic code found at the murders, and eight months later, were finding it progressively more time-consuming to track down all those who lived or worked in that area. Eventually, on 18 September 1987, the police were informed about a chance conversation in a public house where a man named Ian Kelly admitted to having given a blood test on behalf of a work colleague, Colin Pitchfork, who had claimed to be scared of the police. This sample had therefore been given on the basis of a false identity. After many months of pressure on the police and the families of the murder victims, the case was finally broken, as Mr Thomas' report explained:

> ... Also on 19th September 1987, KELLY was arrested and fully admitted in tape recorded interviews that he had attended Danemill Primary School on 27th January 1987 and supplied blood and saliva samples purporting to be Colin PITCHFORK and he used a false passport

supplied by PITCHFORK to confirm his identity as PITCHFORK to the police. These samples were supplied at the instigation of PITCHFORK, and KELLY fully understood that the samples were required in order to eliminate PITCHFORK from a murder enquiry.

36. On 19th September 1987, PITCHFORK was arrested at his home address on suspicion of the murder of Dawn ASHWORTH by the witness Detective Inspector THOMAS, the reporting officer, and Detective Sergeant MASON. When asked in the kitchen of his home address 'Why Dawn ASHWORTH?' PITCHFORK replied, 'Opportunity. She was there and I was there.'

At the police station, Colin Pitchfork admitted the murder of the two teenagers, and his DNA sample confirmed him as the real perpetrator. He pleaded guilty and was sentenced to life imprisonment at Leicester Crown Court on 22 January 1988. DNA had proved both innocence and guilt in this landmark case.

Colin Pitchfork was not the first person to be convicted on DNA evidence because the new technique had already begun to be used to solve a number of cases. There is a possibility that a DNA paternity test was responsible for the criminal conviction of a man for unlawful sexual intercourse at the Old Bailey in the late summer of 1987, as mentioned in *The Blooding* by Joseph Wambaugh (Bantam, 1989), but the case most frequently acknowledged as the first DNA-based conviction was that of Robert Melias, who was convicted of rape in Bristol on 13 November 1987, two months before Colin Pitchfork's conviction.

Robert Melias, a heavy drinker with a number of convictions for burglary, was arrested in August 1987, and a sample of his DNA taken during the course of that arrest was found to match a sample taken in January, earlier that year, from a rape crime scene at Bristol. The scientists calculated that the chance that the rape sample had not come from Melias was one in 4 million of the male population. Melias decided to plead guilty two days before his trial when faced with the damning evidence of the DNA test, and was jailed for eight years. The officer, Constable Clive Tippetts, achieved world-wide recognition for the historical significance of Robert Melias' conviction.

The murder of 22-year-old Lorraine Benson in 1988 in a stranger attack was solved by DNA. She had been to a party in Clapham on 19 December and then went to Raynes Park, where she was due to spend the night with a friend. She never arrived at her friend's house, and was later found strangled to death. Traces of saliva found on her body could not be blood-grouped by Scotland Yard's forensic science laboratory, but were passed on to the lab's new DNA unit, which had only opened that month. (Prior to this, a company called Cellmark Diagnostics had undertaken the Metropolitan Police's DNA analysis cases.) A folded man's handkerchief found at the scene provided a sample of blood that was proved to belong to the victim Lorraine Benson. There was also a yellow crusty stain that proved to be mucus from the suspect's nose. A DNA profile was obtained from this, the first time that DNA from a nasal discharge had been used in a criminal case. There were some strange scratches on the side of a Vauxhall car at the scene, some of which were eventually found to correspond with the zip of Lorraine Benson's jacket.

In February 1989, John Dunne, who lived near the scene of the murder, was arrested for a case of attempted rape, again near Raynes Park station, after his fingerprints had been found at the scene. The initial analysis showed that his DNA matched that of Lorraine Benson's attacker with a probability of one in several hundred, but an impression of his teeth fully matched a bite mark on Lorraine Benson's arm. A full DNA result then showed that the chance of the murderer not being Dunne was 1 in 1.5 million. He pleaded guilty to the murder and was sentenced to life imprisonment. A zip on Dunne's jacket was found to be consistent with the remaining unexplained pattern of scratches found on the Vauxhall car.

This case was the first to be solved by obtaining DNA from nasal secretions, and was the first murder solved by DNA by Scotland Yard's laboratory.

The first database of criminals' DNA was set up by the Forensic Science Service in 1995, and by 1999, matches between crime scenes and suspects had reached about 500 per week, many of them connected with burglary and other crimes not involving violence. As more samples have been added to the database, the heredity basis of DNA has made it possible to direct inquiries towards people whose DNA does not match the sample found at the scene, but where they must have a family relationship with the person who was at the scene. This is a significant advantage over fingerprints, which do not normally have such linkages. Likewise genealogists have sometimes been able to establish from a person's DNA profile that they share a common genetic link with certain parts of the world where their ancestors originated.

JAMES HANRATTY

Forensic science has now advanced to the point where samples can be analysed from exhibits in unsolved cases many years old. Perhaps the classic case is that of James Hanratty, convicted and hanged in 1962 for murdering Michael Gregsten in the A6 murder case. A campaign was fought for many years to clear Hanratty's name and in 2001 his body was exhumed for the purpose of obtaining a DNA sample. This was then compared with DNA extracted from exhibits in the case. Hanratty's DNA, and nobody else's, was found on two exhibits from the scene of the crime. The lawyers arguing the appeal on Hanratty's behalf claimed that the DNA findings could have been the result of contamination of the samples, but the judges at the Court of Appeal decisively rejected their posthumous plea for the quashing of the conviction that had caused so much controversy over the killer's identity.

CHAPTER FOUR

Identity parades:
picking out the guilty

The potential for controversy in the affairs of the royal family is not new. When the Prince of Wales (later George IV) married Queen Caroline of Brunswick in 1795, he had already secretly married Maria FitzHerbert, who, as a Roman Catholic, was prevented from succession to the throne. Despite the birth of their daughter, Princess Charlotte, the marriage was not to George's liking, and he accused Caroline, not without hypocrisy, of adultery. Caroline was turned away from the door of Westminster Abbey at the coronation of her husband as George IV in 1821, and she died later that year. Her funeral procession to Harwich started out from Hammersmith on 14 August 1821, and caused serious public disorder, which eventually led to what was probably the first identification parade on record.

The Prime Minister, Lord Liverpool, ordered the procession to be escorted by the 1st Regiment of the Life Guards and not to go through the City of London because of fears of rioting. There was serious disagreement about these arrangements and conflict started even before the procession began:

> Mr Bailey, of Mount Street, Grosvenor Square, who had been appointed conductor of her Majesty's funeral, arrived at Brandenburg House soon after 5 o'clock, preceded by the hearse, drawn by eight horses, and the mourning coaches...
>
> On the body of her Majesty being demanded of the executors,

Dr LUSHINGTON spoke to the following effect, 'Sir George Nayler and Mr Bailey, you know what has already taken place on the subject of her Majesty's internment... I enter into a solemn protest against the removal of her Majesty's body, in right of the legal power which is vested in me by her late Majesty as executor...'

Mr BAILEY – 'I have orders from Government to remove the body, which is now in the custody of the Lord Chamberlain. I must do my duty. The body must be removed.'

Dr LUSHINGTON – 'Touch the body at your peril...'

The Times, 15 August 1821

Vast crowds wanted to see the procession, despite the pouring rain. A mixture of sympathy for the dead Queen, rumour, a lack of communication, poor crowd control arrangements, and popular hostility to the Government's desire to see the coffin of the Queen leave the country without regard for public sentiment, all led to the route of the procession becoming a contentious flash point. The crowds erected barricades to change the route, and the procession was halted at Oxford Street. The military escort tried to push on to comply with their orders, but the crowd wanted the procession to go through the City. Stones were thrown, and while the soldiers were attempting to clear the barricades, shots were apparently heard. The soldiers opened fire, and two men, Richard Hanney (or Hannay or Honey) and George Francis, were killed.

An inquest into the death of Richard Hanney was later set up under the direction of the coroner, Mr Stirling, and the jury were keen to identify which one of the soldiers had fired the shot that killed him. One of the witnesses, William Alexander, was reported in *The Times* of 18 August 1821 as stating that he 'saw an officer – for so he seemed to be – whom I should know if I was to see him again, from a hundred others... The officer presented his pistol and fired it at the man ... and no sooner was it fired than the man fell down. I saw the pistol go off...'

The jury asked the coroner to make arrangements for witnesses to inspect the soldiers who had been on duty at that location. They were to be dressed in the same way and riding the same horses as on the day of the funeral procession. Arrangements were duly made for the whole of the 1st Regiment of Life Guards to parade at 2pm on 20 August 1821. Proceedings were supervised by Richard Birnie, a Bow Street magistrate, assisted by a colleague, Robert Raynsford. Witnesses passed along the line separately, were instructed not to communicate with each other, and left by a separate entrance. These instructions later became standard procedures for identification parades.

Seven witnesses pointed to individual soldiers to make an identification of sorts, and some made direct accusations, including William Alexander, who said of one soldier, 'I saw him fire a pistol before Mr Honey was laying dead'. Mr Alexander then confirmed his identification to the inquest. These identifications did not lead to a prosecution, however, partly because the soldiers who were picked out denied their involvement to the inquest jury, who eventually returned a verdict of 'Murder by an officer to the jury unknown'. The Life Guards had to accept public condemnation for trying to implement the Prime Minister's orders about the procession route in the face of violent public opposition.

Identification procedures adopted by magistrates were not always as fair as this. Henry Goddard, a Bow Street officer, described in his memoirs the case of the highway robbery and murder of Mr Richardson of Bletchingly, Surrey on 26 February 1834. Earlier that day, Mr Richardson had drawn the attention of the toll gate-keeper at Tadworth to two suspicious men whom he had seen in the vicinity. Because of fear of robbery, he was in the habit of driving with one hand holding the reins, while holding a loaded pistol in the other, and keeping another loaded pistol in reserve.

A suspect, by the name of Sam Cotterell of Bethnal Green, was brought to Epsom Court by Ellis, a Bow Street officer. One of the magistrates suggested that the suspect, unaccompanied by anybody else in a line-up, should dress in a billy-cock [a bowler hat] and a frock to resemble the clothing described by witnesses, which Goddard thought to be very unfair. Fortunately, the witnesses did not identify him, and he was discharged from the court and reimbursed for his expenses and inconvenience. Had he been picked out, he might have been sent for trial, and if found guilty, he would have been executed.

Goddard's fears about this identification process were vindicated when an entirely different suspect, John Young, confessed to the murder after having been sentenced to death at Winchester Assizes on a completely different burglary charge. He said that he had opened fire as a response to Mr Richardson's bold resistance to his attempted highway robbery.

THE CORAM STREET MURDER

Identification could still be contentious, even when an identification parade had been conducted fairly. The murder of 27-year-old Harriet Buswell (alias Clara Burton) at 12 Great Coram Street WC1 in 1872 created enormous controversy (see plate 8). The victim had left her lodgings at about 10pm on Christmas Eve, after borrowing a shilling (5p) from a fellow lodger, and had returned with a male guest, supposedly a German, at about midnight. She had brought with her some bags of apples, oranges and nuts, and was then able to pay her landlady half a sovereign (50p).

The man was heard to leave the house at 6.30am on Christmas morning. At about midday, other occupants of the house, concerned about not seeing her, opened her room and found that the unfortunate Harriet had been brutally murdered. Superintendent Thompson of E Division took charge of the investigation. There was a distinct blood-stained thumb print on the dead woman's forehead, and other blood stains in the room that would have enabled modern detectives to have used forensic evidence to confirm or disprove the identification of any suspects, but, in 1872, those techniques had not yet been introduced. The police did, however, request a Mr Orside to photograph the body in St Giles's workhouse to assist in the issue of identification.

Two barmaid acquaintances had seen Harriet Buswell returning home by bus from the Alhambra Theatre with the man. They described him as a foreigner, about 5 feet 9 inches tall, with a swarthy complexion and blotches or pimples on his face, wearing a dark brown overcoat and a billy-cock hat. A small amount of Harriet Buswell's property was found to be missing: a red morocco purse, a pair of earrings, a brooch, and – a graphic indication of her poverty – a pawn ticket for five pairs of ladies drawers. Harriet Buswell had a small daughter who had been fostered out to a neighbour on payment of 5 shillings (25p) a week. A reward of £200 was issued for information.

The suspicion that the murderer was a foreigner led to the Ramsgate police suspecting Carl Wohlebbe, the assistant surgeon of a German brig *Wangerland,* which had been in port undergoing repairs during the Christmas period. Superintendent James Thomson therefore sent Inspector Harnett down to Ramsgate to check on the identity of the suspect. He took with him George Fleck, the greengrocer who had served Harriet Buswell her nuts and oranges, and Mr Stalker, a waiter from the Alhambra who had served the couple on Christmas Eve.

Carl Wohlebbe, who had indeed visited London over Christmas, was arrested and paraded amongst some 20 members of the ship's crew before the witnesses, but both witnesses stated that he was not the man who had spent the evening with Harriet Buswell. Amongst the other members of the ship's company, however, the witnesses did see the ship's chaplain, Dr Gottfried Hessel, who had also been to London at the same time, and they positively identified him as the culprit. Dr Hessel was therefore arrested and charged with the murder.

On 20 January 1873, Dr Hessel appeared before Bow Street magistrates court. Superintendent Thomson proved that Hessel had been in London on the night in question, and the identification of the two witnesses at Ramsgate was sufficient for him to be remanded in custody. After the hearing, the police sought legal assistance, and a firm of solicitors was appointed to instruct a barrister to conduct the prosecution. Sir Richard Mayne had died three years earlier, and had been replaced by a military man, Colonel Sir Edmund Henderson, so the days of a barrister Commissioner supervising cases in detail were over. This early involvement of lawyers to assist the police in conducting the prosecution was a forerunner of the role of the Director of Public Prosecutions and the Crown Prosecution Service.

When Dr Hessel appeared at Bow Street the following week, two other witnesses also identified him in the dock, but others were not sure. A housemaid from the Royal Hotel in Ramsgate testified that Dr Hessel had asked for some turpentine and a clothes brush when he had returned from London after Christmas, and there was also evidence that one of Dr Hessel's handkerchiefs had been saturated with blood.

Dr Hessel, however, gave alibi evidence that because of illness he had never left his London hotel on the night in question, and he was supported by Carl Wohlebbe. Despite the case being conducted by lawyers, the police had apparently not been asked to interview witnesses to investigate this alibi. The magistrate, Mr Vaughan, discharged Dr Hessel from the court, declaring that he was being released without suspicion. The case generated enormous publicity. Dr Hessel was cheered by the crowds and a public subscription was raised for him by *The Daily Telegraph,* before his departure for Brazil.

The police never did prove who had spent the night with Harriet Buswell. The investigation was criticized, in particular the decision to make inquiries amongst the men who had been involved with Harriet in the past, an initiative that may have challenged Victorian attitudes to prostitution. When Dr Hessel was acquitted, the idea of a respectable gentleman being wrongly accused of such a crime reignited the newspapers' outrage, despite the Bow Street magistrate's comments that the action of the police had been justified after Dr Hessel had been so clearly identified. *The Times* wrote:

> A cruel injury has been inflicted on Dr Hessel without the slightest justification. To a man of character and feeling, nothing can be more painful than to be accused of so horrid a charge, and to have to submit to a week's detention and to a prolonged examination in court...
>
> Such a blunder is a disgrace to our system of criminal prosecution, and it is to be regretted the Magistrate should have thought it necessary to say a single word in exculpation of the Police. This is simply a culmination of a long course of blundering in respect to the Coram-street murder, and it probably illustrates the error which has been committed throughout. If the Police are capable of being led away on a false scent by such trivial evidence as that on which they arrested Dr Hessel, what probability is there that they pursued their investigations from the first with any sagacity? ... Let us hope they will at least be more careful in the future, and that they will recognize the fact that they have adopted a completely fallacious principle of investigation.
>
> *The Times,* 31 January 1873

But not everybody viewed Dr Hessel as an innocent clergyman. Shortly after-wards, a letter was received from Germany, exposing a less reputable side of his life, but as the author(s) were anonymous and Dr Hessel had by that time been acquitted, no account could be taken of it, nor could its true significance be assessed:

> In how far Dr Hessel now undergoing examination for murder is guilty of that act will the examination soon show, but we think it to be our duty to give a short history of the accused & his wife...
>
> Dr Hessel was for about 2 or 3 years employed as a reformed preacher at the New Peters Church, the last year of which he also kept a boys school to increase his income, the salary for his pastoral duties not being sufficient to keep up his position in Society.
>
> By his good address & gentlemanly appearance, he introduced himself into the best society (this could only be of short duration); as he as well as his wife contracted debts, which only could be recovered by legal proceedings. To this we have to add his profligate & spendthrift conduct; he used to be drunk late at night & early in the morning, which can be proved by his servants, & used to borrow money wherever he could. This brought him, of course, so low that he could not pay his rent & not having any more articles to pledge, he saw himself obliged to give in his resignation to the Senioren College to search for better luck in a foreign country (Bahaia). His resignation was willingly granted as all his behaviour & conduct was fully known, & the Senioren College granted him, at his request, the substantial assistance in the sum of 180 thalers to pay small debts of honour which he did not pay. To complete this disgraceful career, during the last days of his stay here he gave dinner to his boon companions from which he & his wife disappeared & left them to pay the expenses to his memory.
>
> All that he & his wife possessed was principally borrowed, the smallest part of which was paid by cheques, so that in all he leaves now a debt of several thousand thalers. To the truthfulness of these statements which Dr Hessel cannot deny, we refer you to the Senioren College of the reformed parish, as also to the Royal Court of Public Examination here.
>
> MEPO 3/80

ATTEMPTING TO IMPROVE THE IDENTIFICATION PROCESS

Nearly six years after the hunt for Harriet Buswell's killer had caused such controversy, Inspector Abberline, who would later play an important role in the Whitechapel Murder investigations (see Chapter 6) was called upon to deal with a judge's criticism of the practice of placing police officers in an identification parade alongside the suspect.

Abberline reported that on 3 December 1878, Arthur Saville appeared at Middlesex Sessions, accused of indecent exposure. PC Cranes had arrested him, and the female witness had picked him out from an identification parade that had included nine other men. Only two of the nine were private citizens, however; the remainder were police officers. This practice, which would be regarded as very improper today and would probably be seen as unfair, even when compared to the Life Guards' identification parade 57 years earlier, contravened the principle that the members of the parade alongside the suspect should be of similar build, appearance and position in life. But the Home Office was extremely reluctant to make any binding regulations restricting police officers appearing on these parades, simply because of the great difficulty in persuading the public to co-operate by voluntarily attending a police station for this purpose. Public reluctance to become involved might have been due to the disquiet that still reverberated from the result of Dr Hessel joining the Ramsgate identification parade six years earlier.

In 1882, Howard Vincent, who had been appointed as Director of Criminal Intelligence four years earlier, compiled his *Police Code* for police officers about law and procedure, which stipulated that the identification parade process should be conducted in the fairest possible manner, and that the suspect should be placed with five or six others 'of as nearly as possible similar appearance as to age, clothes and position in life'. Eventually the practice of placing police officers in a parade to make up a sufficient number was prohibited, and it became standard to place eight or more members of the public alongside a suspect. This remained the recognized procedure until modern times, with one-way glass screens eventually being introduced to assist witnesses who might be nervous or frightened. In the twenty-first century, the whole process is often undertaken by witnesses viewing a video clip of the suspect in amongst a series of other films taken from a comprehensive library of people of similar appearance.

In 1922, two famous detectives, Percy Savage, then the Divisional Detective Inspector responsible for Kensington (F Division), and Superintendent (later a CID chief constable) Frederick Wensley reported their concerns about prisoners indulging in various ruses to change their appearance in the period between their arrest and identification parades. One man had his moustache shaved off in Brixton prison, another man replaced his smart collar and tie with a soiled handkerchief around his neck, whilst others took out their false teeth, removed wigs, and even, in one case, wore an inflatable rubber chest protector that could be inflated or deflated to alter his chest size.

THE CASE OF ADOLF BECK

The years around the turn of the 20th century provided a more notorious case of mistaken identity than Dr Hessel's. Adolf Beck (see plate 10) was arrested on two occasions, in 1896 and 1904, after female victims of fraud had wrongly identified him in the street. On both occasions more frauds by the same method had occured, and further victims also wrongly picked him out on formal identification parades. Beck was imprisoned in 1896 on identification and handwriting evidence. He was also regarded as the person who had been convicted of similar frauds in 1877 in the name of John Smith. Eventually, in 1904, whilst Beck was in prison awaiting sentence for his second wrongful conviction, the real offender played the same trick on two other women and, by good fortune, was immediately arrested. Beck at last had a cast-iron alibi because this time he was in prison and the identity of the other man could be established.

The case was summarized in an Appendix to a Cabinet paper presented on 7 December 1904 by Viscount Chilston, the Home Secretary of the day:

> In 1877 a series of frauds on loose women took place. In each case a man
> called on a woman, said he was a wealthy Lord, wanted her to live with
> him or go yachting with him, said she required better clothes, gave her
> a cheque for a large sum to purchase them, said he wished to give her a

new ring, borrowed a ring from her as a pattern, and having gone off with the ring, disappeared. A German named Weiss was convicted of these frauds in the name of John Smith. He was undoubtedly guilty, and served a term of five years.

In 1895 a series of exactly similar frauds occurred; about 50 women were defrauded. One of the women walking in Victoria Street saw a man whom she believed to be the swindler and gave him in charge. This man was Adolf Beck. Of 22 women brought to see him, 10 positively identified him as the swindler; of the others some were uncertain, and one at least said he was not the man. The police believed him to be the same person as John Smith of 1877 and he was tried on 10 charges of fraud. The belief of the prosecution was that he was the same person as John Smith, whose *modus operandi* was precisely similar, and whose writing on the cheques and notes was curiously similar, but this was not gone into at the trial.

The defence would have been that the frauds of 1895 must have been committed by the John Smith of 1877, but that Beck was not Smith, and they were ready to prove that Beck was in South America when Smith was convicted and imprisoned in England. The Common Sergeant (Sir Forrest Fulton) refused to allow the defence to give evidence for this purpose, and as the count charging Beck with Smith's previous convictions was dropped by the prosecution, the question whether Beck was Smith was not tried.

Beck was convicted on the evidence (1) of 10 women who swore positively that he was the man who had swindled them; and (2) on the evidence of Gurrin, the expert, who said that the writing on the cheques and notes given by the swindler was that of Beck, disguised. Beck was sentenced to seven years' penal servitude.

While he was in prison he consistently asserted that he was not John Smith and that he was innocent of the frauds of 1895. The question of his identity with John Smith was inquired into by the Home Office in 1898, and his description and marks were compared with those of John Smith now brought forward for the first time. They were found not to correspond, and in particular it was found that Smith was circumcised, while Beck was not. The Home Office decided that Beck was not John Smith, and Smith's name and conviction was erased from his penal record. Sir Forrest Fulton, who was consulted, advised that the question of whether he was Smith or not was immaterial; the point, he said, had been excluded at the trial, and Beck had been convicted of the 1895 frauds by overwhelming evidence. His petition for release was therefore refused. In 1901, Beck was released on licence, when he had served his full time.

In 1904 frauds on prostitutes recommenced, the *modus operandi* being exactly as before. The police told one of the women to stand in Tottenham Court Road, near the place where Beck was lodging, and, as he went in the morning to the City, she identified him as the person who swindled her, and gave him in charge. All the five women who had been defrauded picked him out and identified him. He was tried at the Central Criminal Court in May, and on the evidence of the five women and of Gurrin, who again said the writing was that of Beck, disguised, he was convicted, but sentence was deferred until the July Sessions of the Central Criminal Court.

While Beck was in prison awaiting sentence, another case of fraud occurred, the swindler following the same device. He obtained two rings from two girls of the name of Turner, but, their suspicions being aroused, he was followed and arrested while pawning the rings.

He was identified beyond doubt as the John Smith of 1877: it was clearly established that he, and not Beck, was the swindler in all the 1904 frauds; and there was the strongest possible presumption that he, and not Beck, was responsible also for those of 1896. This presumption becomes a certainty when the cheques given by Smith in 1877 are compared with those given by the swindler in 1896, and the identity of handwriting is recognised.

Mr Beck was released and granted a Free Pardon in respect of his convictions.   CAB 37/73/160

Beck was prosecuted because of the peculiar and consistent method of the frauds, his similarity in appearance to the real offender, the opinion of a handwriting expert, and a succession of female victims who identified him for two prosecutions. The recollections of the women may have been at fault, but they were in good company. The police officer who had originally arrested John Smith in 1877 gave evidence at the magistrates court that Adolf Beck was the same man, and the prosecuting counsel at the Old Bailey in the 1877 John Smith case was the trial judge, Sir Forrest Fulton, who dealt with Adolf Beck's first trial in 1896.

The real John Smith was caught on 7 July 1904, when, in the name of William Thomas, he used the same fraud method against two sisters, Violet and Beulah Turner, who, having lent him their rings, asked their landlord, Fritz Glenville, to follow him. Glenville saw that the man went to a pawn-broker to dispose of his tenants' rings and called the police. There was a continuous chain of evidence linking the suspect to the crime, and William Thomas was later sentenced to five years' imprisonment.

The credit for resolving this miscarriage of justice lay firstly with the 1904 trial judge, Mr Justice Grantham, who had lingering doubts about Beck's guilt and had delayed concluding the case, despite apparently strong pros-ecution evidence and procedures. It was in this period of delay, before being sentenced, that the crucial arrest of the real offender took place. Much credit is also due to Inspector John Kane for his action in making a series of formal reports to investigate William Thomas thoroughly, and to establish that he was the same man as the John Smith who had been convicted in 1877.

Kane had been in court during Beck's 1896 trial and knew that it had been accepted that the handwriting in the 1877 and the 1896 frauds was identical. The question was whether the handwriting expert was right to claim that it was Beck's writing in disguise. Kane examined the writing of the recent prisoner William Thomas and found that it was strikingly similar to the letters on which Beck had been convicted. Beck was Norwegian, and had claimed that the fraudster was a German. John Kane established that the real identity of John Smith, alias William Thomas, was a German, or Austrian, named William Weiss. He brought three of the witnesses who had identified Beck to an identification parade, and they unhesitatingly picked out Weiss as the culprit. This proved Beck's innocence, and he was awarded £5,000 compensation for the miscarriage of justice he had suffered.

The judgement of the handwriting expert Thomas Gurrin had proved to be as fallible as the recollection of some of the witnesses, and there was no system such as fingerprinting yet in operation to verify a prisoner's record. No matter how persuasively Beck might have complained about the miscarriage of justice, there was, at that time, no legal means of appealing against his conviction by a jury, notwithstanding that, in 1898, the Home Office had accepted that he was not the same man as John Smith who had been convicted in 1877. His case was instrumental in bringing about the introduction of the Court of Criminal Appeal in 1907 as a tribunal for deciding upon such cases.

Adolf Beck was not the first, nor the last victim of a miscarriage of justice, and the courts have, over the years, developed a healthy scepticism of uncorroborated identification evidence by witnesses.

CHAPTER FIVE

Press and TV appeals:
helping police with their inquiries

In 1881, seven years before the Whitechapel Murders would make 'Jack the Ripper' infamous, Howard Vincent had been Director of Criminal Intelligence at Scotland Yard for over three years. He was rapidly reorganizing the detective functions of what had become the Criminal Investigation Department, and improving the circulation of information about wanted criminals. In fact, the extent to which he used press advertisements in the hunt for fugitives earned him a reprimand from the Home Office, who apparently regarded the practice as undignified.

On 27 June 1881, another murder was committed on the railway, this time on the train from London Bridge to Brighton. Although it occurred outside the Metropolitan Police District, Vincent nevertheless became heavily involved in the case and demonstrated the power of newspapers to help the police track down wanted criminals.

THE MURDER OF ISAAC GOLD

In an age when individual travellers were often remembered by the railway staff, William Franks, one of three ticket collectors at London Bridge, described the departure on that day of a regular traveller and coin dealer by the name of Isaac Gold. Franks knew that Gold generally travelled from London Bridge on the 2pm express to Brighton, and greeted his passenger, who had been walking up and down the platform prior to boarding the train. Franks recalled how Isaac Gold had entered a first-class smoking compartment of the third carriage, in a seat facing the engine. He also remembered a younger man, who appeared to be looking for somebody already on the train. Later, it was discovered that his name was Percy LeFroy Mapleton. The young man passed Gold's compartment, hesitated by the next compartment occupied by a young lady, then turned sharply round and tried to open the carriage door so as to sit in the same compartment as Gold. Franks opened the door for him and inspected his ticket. The ticket collector could therefore testify that Isaac Gold left London Bridge with nobody else in his compartment except for the young man.

At the next stop, East Croydon, a porter confirmed that only three people, all ladies, entered the first-class section of the train, and it was therefore established that Isaac Gold and Mapleton were the only occupants of their compartment on the non-stop journey from East Croydon to Preston Park. The guard on the train, Thomas Watson, described the train's journey, and what happened when they arrived at Preston Park:

> When we stopped at Preston Park, I saw Gibson the ticket collector on the platform and he called my attention to a gentleman he was talking to – that was the prisoner. They were both on the platform. I went up to them. The prisoner had no hat on and all his flesh that I could see was smothered with blood. I did not notice his clothes. I asked him what was the matter and he said, 'I have been cruelly treated on the way. There have been two other people in this compartment that have attempted to murder and rob me and they have got out on the way.'...
>
> I noticed a piece of an old-fashioned watch chain that looked like gold hanging from his shoe. I said 'What have you got here?' and immediately took hold of the chain and pulled it out. When I pulled the chain, a gold watch attached to the chain came out of the shoe... He said 'I know nothing about it.'...
>
> On arriving at Brighton ... I left my brake and went through the first-class compartment that the prisoner had been sitting in... I found two flash sovereigns – one under the seat on the floor and one as if it had fallen through the hole of the rope mat on to the floor. ASSI 36/26

In his dishevelled and blood-stained condition, Mapleton, also known as Percy LeFroy, was clearly in need of medical treatment, but the fact of the watch and chain being kept in his shoe made his story of being attacked very odd. He was taken further down the line to Brighton, escorted by the ticket collector at Preston Park. At Brighton station, Mapleton, an unsuccessful journalist, told the station master and Police Inspector Gibson that he had been shot and wounded during his journey. He was searched and was found to have two Hanoverian medals in his pockets, similar to those found earlier by Thomas Watson in the blood-stained railway carriage.

Nobody was satisfied with Mapleton's account of himself, but, presuming that nobody had left the moving carriage after the train's last stop at East Croydon, the police concluded that the young man might have been attempting suicide, which was then a criminal offence. He was taken to the police station where Detective Constable Howland interviewed him and took details of his alleged assailants, before passing him on to the hospital where his wounds were treated. Then, as a precaution, he was taken back to his home in Wallington, Surrey by Detective Sergeant George Holmes. During this journey, a telegram from the station master at Balcombe arrived, changing the situation dramatically. It read 'Man found dead this afternoon in tunnel here. Name on papers "I Gold". He is now lying here. Reply quick.'

Isaac Gold's body had been found beside the railway track near the Balcombe tunnel, 32 miles from London. He had been shot in the neck and stabbed in the chest. His watch was missing. In due course, Mapleton's collar and Isaac Gold's hat, purse and umbrella, but no gun, were found at various places beside the railway line between Balcombe and Preston Park. The incident turned into a murder inquiry, with Mapleton as the prime suspect.

Detective Sergeant Holmes remained oblivious of these developments, however, and his statement described his role in what turned out to be a most unfortunate episode for the police:

I … am a detective officer in the employment of the Brighton railway. I am still attached to the Metropolitan Police force… At Haywards Heath … I asked him [the prisoner] if he was in the habit of carrying firearms and he said, 'No. I like to keep a good distance from those things.' Balcombe was the next stopping place, and there Howland gave me some information. I returned to the carriage where the prisoner was and Mr Brown, the Station Master at Three Bridges got into the carriage there… He spoke very loud and said a man had been found dead in the tunnel. I said, 'Don't speak so loud as the man is listening.'

At Croydon … the prisoner and I got into the cab… We stopped about two houses short of the prisoner's house… He asked me into the drawing room… He then made a statement which I took down in writing… I asked him the number of his watch… The prisoner said the number of his watch was 56312. I said I should like to see it. He then took the watch from, I believe, his trousers pocket. He gave it to me in my hand. I opened it and I said, 'You have given the wrong number. It's 16261'. He said, 'Yes. I have made a mistake.'… I asked him where we should see him tomorrow in case we obtained any information and he said he would be at Wallington till 12 and after that at the United Hearts Club, Surrey Street, Strand. I was in there about half an hour. Prisoner let me out of the house and bade me good night… I left and went to Wallington station. I there received a telegram from the Station Master, and in consequence I returned at once to the prisoner's house. I was about 6 to 7 minutes from the time I left till the time I returned.   ASSI 36/26

Holmes had duly checked the number of Mapleton's watch (which was subsequently proved to belong to Isaac Gold) as requested by his senior officer, but the telegram he received on his return to Wallington station specifically instructed him not to let Mapleton out of his sight and custody. He therefore returned to the address with understandable haste, but then waited until colleagues arrived as reinforcements. Two officers went into the house, and Detective Constable Howland went to the rear to block off any escape, whilst Holmes watched the front of the premises. Their care in surrounding the house was to no avail, however: Mapleton had vanished, telling a servant in the house that he was going to visit the doctor. The inquest on Isaac Gold was the occasion for severe criticism of Detective Sergeant Holmes for failing to keep hold of the suspect.

Howard Vincent had taken up a helpful interest in the murder, which had occurred just outside his geographical area of jurisdiction, but this became far more intense when he learnt that the hapless Holmes was in fact one of his own Metropolitan Police officers attached to the railway company. Detective Inspectors Donald Swanson (later to take a prominent role in investigating the Whitechapel Murders) and Frederick Jarvis of Scotland Yard were assigned to the case. There was much pressure to rescue the situation.

Vincent made a special request to the press for their help, and the *Daily Telegraph* published the police description of Mapleton (see plate 11):

> Age 22, middle height, very thin, sickly appearance, scratches on throat, wounds on head, probably clean shaved, low felt hat, black coat, teeth much discoloured.

In an age when images of people were rarely seen, the Victorians were often far more adept at describing people verbally than we could probably manage today, and the Mapleton case gave the *Daily Telegraph* much scope for expanding on the police description more graphically:

> He is very round shouldered, and his thin overcoat hangs in awkward folds about his spare figure. His forehead and chin are both receding. He has a slight moustache, and very small dark whiskers. His jawbones are prominent, his cheeks sunken and sallow, and his teeth fully exposed when laughing. His upper lip is thin and drawn inwards. His eyes are grey and large. His gait is singular; he is inclined to slouch and when not carrying a bag, his left hand is usually in his pocket. He generally carries a crutch stick. *Daily Telegraph,* 1 July 1881

Far more significantly, the *Daily Telegraph* published an artist's impression of Mapleton by asking the assistance of a person who knew the young man well. This was the first time that such a picture had been used in this way by any newspaper and it created enormous public interest. As a result, a number of arrests took place, including a passenger on the mail train from Paddington to Devon, a man in Sevenoaks who was actually charged with the murder until somebody who knew the real Mapleton eliminated him, and another suspect as far away as Calais.

On 8 July, 11 days after the murder, Mapleton was finally arrested in Stepney, East London. Attention turned to who would be entitled to claim a share in the £200 reward that had been offered for information leading to his arrest. Mapleton's new landlady, Mrs Bickers, had started to worry about the behaviour of her new tenant who remained permanently in his room, and she knew that another of her lodgers had spoken to a friend about the strange man who had just arrived at the house. Anxious about receiving her rent, she claimed the reward on the basis that she herself was the origin of the tip-off, despite the fact that she had not seen the picture in the *Daily Telegraph.*

However, it was the arresting officer, Donald Swanson, who reported the true sequence of events. He related how a man with no apparent connection to Mrs Bickers and her lodger had come to Scotland Yard and given him Mrs Bickers' address as the place where he would find his quarry:

> I beg to report with reference to the attached letter from Mrs Bickers of No 1 Jamaica Street, Stepney … that about 7pm on 8th July I met two young men, unknown to me, in Scotland Yard… They had some information respecting Percy Mapleton which they desired to give the officer in charge of the Criminal Investigation Dept… The informant, who gave his name as D. Mugford of No 25 New Union Street, said, in substance – There is a reward of £200 offered for the arrest of Percy LeFroy Mapleton. What guarantee have we that the reward will be paid us if we give the information that will lead to his arrest? …
>
> 'We have reason to believe that a person calling himself G. Clark who has lodged at 32 Smith Street Stepney ever since the night of the murder, and who has not been out of the house since, is Percy LeFroy Mapleton… We must decline to tell you from what source we derived our information but we have <u>good</u> reason to believe that the person is LeFroy.'
>
> Inspector Jarvis and I then left and went to 32 Smith Street, Stepney,

> where we apprehended LeFroy, who had been passing under the name of G. Clark so that Mugford's information was correct.   HO144/83/A6404

Percy LeFroy Mapleton appeared before Lord Coleridge at Maidstone Winter Assizes, being prosecuted by the Attorney-General, assisted by Mr Poland, the barrister who had appeared at Bow Street Magistrates Court in the case against Dr Gottfried Hessel nearly nine years earlier.

The evidence clearly showed that nobody else but Mapleton had been in the same compartment as Isaac Gold, that the watch found in the prisoner's sock belonged to his victim, that Mapleton had been short of money, and that he had pawned and, on the morning of the crime, had redeemed a small revolver. Poor Detective Sergeant Holmes gave evidence and had to admit that he had known that there had been a dead body found on the line with no watch, that Mapleton had given the wrong number for the watch found in his possession, that Mapleton had been covered in blood, but had only superficial wounds himself, that, nevertheless, he had left Mapleton at his lodgings, and that he had delayed entering the house to make an arrest until assistance arrived. The watch chain that Mapleton had in his possession when he arrived at Preston Park was missing. The early stages of the investigation did not show the police in a good light.

During Holmes' evidence, the picture printed in the *Daily Telegraph* was produced to the jury, partly to clarify whether it might have influenced witnesses' identification evidence. *The Times* court report of 7 November 1881 stated of their competitor's picture that 'it did not bear any resemblance to the prisoner'.

The evidence against Mapleton was overwhelming, and the jury took only 10 minutes to reach their 'guilty' verdict. Mapleton was convicted and was sentenced to death.

Whilst in Lewes prison, he confessed to another murder, that of a Lieutenant Roper, but he retracted the confession, and there was some suggestion that his actions were only a ruse to delay his execution. He also wrote his autobiography, which the Home Office thought was not suitable for publication. Mapleton's petitions for a reprieve were unsuccessful and he was executed on 30 November 1881 (see plate 12).

The first radio and TV appeals

The first appeal for the public to assist with tracking down a suspect to be broadcast by BBC radio occurred on 9 January 1933. It gave a description of Samuel John Furnace, who was wanted for the murder of Walter Spatchett, whose dead body was found in a shed in Hawley Crescent, Camden Town, London.

The first picture of a suspect wanted for murder to be transmitted by television was, according to *Police Review* of 9 October 1953, the BBC broadcast of a picture of William Pettit. The police wanted to interview him in connection with the murder of Mrs Rene Brown, who was found stabbed to death in a field in Chislehurst, Kent.

The newspapers of the day did their best to satisfy public curiosity about the process of capital punishment, and the *Daily Telegraph*'s special correspondent gave a full account of hangman William Marwood's explanation of the mechanics of his gallows, rope and other paraphernalia. While the bell continued to toll as the 9 o'clock deadline approached, Mapleton arrived from his cell, accompanied by a clergyman, two prison officers, the Under Sheriff, the prison governor, a surgeon and a magistrate. Marwood quickly placed a white linen cap over the condemned prisoner's face, adjusted the noose, and, as soon as the clergyman had completed intoning his rite, pulled the lever of the trap door and consigned Mapleton to his instant death.

The newspaper account reflected their correspondent's misgivings about the ritual involved in capital punishment, which was eventually abolished some 80 years later.

An hour after the execution, an inquest jury assembled at the prison, viewed the body, and then heard formal evidence from the prison governor and the surgeon before reaching their verdict that Percy Mapleton had died from hanging, the final conclusion to a life made forever significant by his picture in a newspaper that had helped police with their inquiries.

PC EDGAR'S MURDER AND *THE BLUE LAMP*

The phrase 'helping police with their inquiries' originated from a case that occurred on 13 February 1948. As a result of several burglaries in the Highgate and Southgate areas of north London, a number of police officers were deployed on special plain-clothes patrols. One of these officers was PC Nathaniel Edgar, who had been patrolling with his partner PC McPartlan. At about 7pm the two police constables followed a suspect, but then lost sight of him. They split up to try to find him, then met up again an hour later, and parted once more to continue their search. It was PC Edgar who found and challenged the man at Wades Hill, Winchmore Hill, and took brief particulars in his pocket book, 'M (or Mr) Thomas Donald, 247 Cambridge Road, Enfield, BEAH 257/2'. The officer's action in making this note proved to be a vital clue in the murder hunt that followed, but it was PC Edgar's last action, because soon afterwards he was shot. He died in the North Middlesex Hospital at 9.30pm that evening, the first officer to have been shot on duty for some years, and the case made a great impression, not only on his colleagues, but also on the public.

Detective Inspector Thomas Stinton's report set out the steps taken to trace the suspect Donald George Thomas, wanted as a deserter since 13 October 1947, and the form of the public statement made by the police became in itself a historic milestone. In 1945, in an attempt to develop better relationships with the Press, Commissioner Sir Harold Scott had recruited a Public Information Officer by name of Percy Fearnley. He had many years' experience of newspapers and as a press officer in the BBC, the War Office and in India. The hunt for PC Edgar's murderer was a good opportunity to enlist the help of the public, but it was also important not to publicize any statement that might prejudice the future trial. After much discussion with Fearnley, a form of words was agreed that stated that 'the police urgently wished to interview Donald George Thomas, who was believed to be able to help them in their inquiries'. Thomas Stinton described the result of that appeal:

> As a result of this widespread publicity, Mr Stanley John Winkless of
> 173 Elmington Road, Camberwell, SE5, notified police at Camberwell

that he knew a man named Donald George Thomas who had visited his home occasionally, that his wife Noreen Winkless had been missing from home for the past three weeks, and that he suspected she was in company of the wanted man...

Late on the afternoon of Monday 16th February ... we were successful in requesting the Press to publish a photograph of the missing woman ... with the result that at 7.30am Mrs Constance Smeed, a boarding house proprietress, of 16 Mayflower Road, Clapham, SW9, noticed in the morning paper the photograph and name of Mrs Winkless, and of our desire to interview her... She suspected that the woman who at that moment was occupying the top front room at their house with a man, was identical with the woman Police desired to interview...

The officers burst into the room, PC Wheeler leading, and saw Thomas running towards a bed which was behind the door. The man leaped on to the bed and dived his hand under the pillow. PC Wheeler flung himself across the lower part of the man on the left side and Inspector Moody threw himself on top of the man and seized his right hand which he had taken from underneath the pillow and was then holding a gun. The man struggled and Inspector Moody pushed the man's right hand up and wrenched the gun from his hand whilst he struggled to escape.

It was then noticed that Mrs Winkless was lying in the bed underneath all three of them. She was allowed to get out of bed and dress... Thomas replied 'That gun's full up and they were all for you, you bastards.   MEPO 3/2998

The information from Stanley Winkless about his wife probably being with Thomas, and the subsequent transfer of attention to the whereabouts of Mrs Winkless, led to the dramatic arrest of Thomas in Clapham. The publication in the newspapers of the tragic murder of PC Edgar, with the information about Donald Thomas and Noreen Winkless, was an excellent example of the ability of newspapers to publicize vital information and to harness the public's willingness to help police solve a very serious crime.

Some weeks later, the Commissioner, Sir Harold Scott, received a letter dated 6 May 1948 from Jan Read, who worked for film magnate J. Arthur

The Tottenham Outrage and the King's Police Medal

The King's Police Medal was instituted by King Edward VII on 7 July 1909, following representations made after an armed robbery, where a number of officers were shot and wounded in a running battle with two Latvian immigrants. Paul Hefeld and Jacob Lepidus stole the wages from Schnurrman's rubber factory on the corner of Tottenham High Road and Chestnut Road on 23 January 1909. The two stood at the corner armed with pistols, and when the chauffeur-driven car carrying the wages clerk drew up, they seized the leather cash bag and shot at the chauffeur and a passing factory worker, who grappled with Lepidus. PCs William Tyler and Albert Newman came running from the nearby police station in Tottenham High Road, and a long chase began, during which the anarchists fired over 400 rounds at their pursuers. A passing housewife threw a potato at them, and an increasing number of police officers joined the chase, some armed with truncheons, and another mounted on a bicycle, brandishing a cutlass.

PC Newman persuaded the chauffeur and original victim of the robbery to run the gunmen down at the Mitchley Road Mission Hall, but this resulted in the car's radiator water pipe being ruined by gunfire, the wounding of the chauffeur, and the death of a 10-year-old boy Ralph Joscelyne.

At the footpath leading to Tottenham Marshes, PC Tyler took a short cut and headed them off, but was shot at point blank range by Hefeld and killed. By this time the pursuers included footballers, labourers, duck shooters and gypsies, but when they reached Chingford Road, the robbers commandeered a tram and forced the conductor to drive it, while the driver hid upstairs. In turn, the police took over a tram going in the opposite direction and reversed it in hot pursuit until the robbers were warned by their conductor of a nearby police station. This caused them to abandon the tram for a milk van, which they wrecked by cornering too fast, and then a greengrocer's horse and van that would only go slowly because they had not released the brake!

After a further chase on foot, Hefeld gave up in a state of exhaustion and shot himself, dying in hospital three weeks later. Lepidus locked himself in a cottage at Oak Hill and shot himself dead just as PCs Charles Eagles, Charles Dixon and John Cater broke in to arrest him.

The incident created enormous public disquiet and soon became known as the Tottenham Outrage. There was enormous sympathy for those killed and injured, matched by admiration, including the King's, for the courage that the police officers and others had displayed. There was no official means of recognizing such gallantry in the police service at the time, but the incident was the catalyst leading to the institution of the King's Police Medal on 7 July 1909 for conspicuous gallantry in saving life and property, or in preventing crime or arresting criminals. The medal could also be awarded for an especially distinguished record in administrative or detective service, success in organizing police forces, or in maintaining their organization in special difficulties. John Cater, Charles Dixon and Charles Eagles were amongst the first officers to whom the medals were awarded.

In the Second World War, the King's Police Medal became the King's Police and Fire Service Medal (KPFSM), principally in recognition of the undoubted heroism shown by Fire Service officers during the War. When the George Cross and George Medal were instituted in 1940, the KPFSM was then reserved for cases not connected with war activities. In 1951, regulations were introduced directing that the George Medal should replace the KPFSM for gallantry, except in posthumous cases. So the George Medal and the KPFSM were seen as broadly equivalent in terms of the degree of gallantry required.

There were 44 awards of the KPFSM to Metropolitan Police officers between 1941 and 1953, and 61% of these medals (in 27 incidents) involved facing firearms, as in the arrest of Donald Thomas. Nowadays the award of a medal to a police officer for an act of courage has become a very rare event, probably because of greater care and planning in operations involving armed criminals, the introduction of protective equipment and the use of specialist firearms officers. It is also true that the pattern of awarding medals for gallantry to police officers has changed. As at May 2006, the last award of a George Medal to a Metropolitan Police officer was in 1992, and the last Queen's Gallantry Medal in 1997.

Rank, seeking Scotland Yard's assistance in making a film about the Metropolitan Police. Reed suggested that it would be very timely because 'a great deal of public sympathy exists for the police in their tackling of the current crime wave, and, if properly made, such a film could show the public how they can co-operate. We should not want to make another film like *Night Beat*, which as it seems to us, used the police as an excuse for yet another cops and robbers story about spivs and the East End. Our idea is to make something much more genuinely about the police force and policemen ...'

The film project became *The Blue Lamp,* one of the most influential films ever made, and the *Evening Standard* of 10 August 1949 later quoted the director Basil Dean as saying that the film had been based on PC Edgar's story. In turn, this led to the long-running TV series *Dixon of Dock Green,* starring Jack Warner.

On 22 February 1949, in another act of recognition of the courage displayed played by police officers in London, the names of the four policemen involved in the arrest of PC Edgar's killer all appeared in the *London Gazette*, a publication regarded by the British government as a uniquely official newspaper, where legal and other formal notices are published. The men had all been awarded the King's Police and Fire Service Medal for gallantry.

The cases described in this chapter, particularly those of Percy LeFroy Mapleton, PC Nat Edgar and the Tottenham Outrage, were all milestones that naturally drew the willing assistance of newspapers, television and film companies to help catch dangerous offenders. They have also served to recognize and portray the courage displayed by police officers thrust into danger whilst doing their duty. Over the years, TV series and films about the police have become commonplace, and the role of the media in publishing details that enable the public to help the police in catching offenders has become universally recognized, not least with the introduction of special TV programmes dealing with appeals for information about crime, such as *Police 5* and *Crimewatch*. This is especially apparent when the public becomes anxious about a particularly horrific incident, or series of crimes.

CHAPTER SIX

Counting corpses:
the challenge of 'Jack the Ripper'

The Whitechapel Murders are a good example of how difficult it is to be certain about which crimes are definitely the work of one man. They also show how anonymous taunting letters or hoaxes can sometimes divert the focus of police inquiries.

EMMA ELIZABETH SMITH

The story of the Whitechapel Murders starts on Tuesday, 3 April 1888 at 1.30 in the morning, when a prostitute, Emma Elizabeth Smith, was badly assaulted in Osborn Street, Whitechapel, by a gang of three men. She died of peritonitis in hospital on the following day, and police were only informed of the incident on 6 April. The victim had said that she had been robbed of her money during the attack. In addition to the internal injuries that caused her death, her head was bruised and her right ear torn. The weapon was a blunt instrument rather than a knife. It was not uncommon for prostitutes to be badly assaulted in Whitechapel at the time; indeed one of Emma Smith's friends had survived a similar attack herself.

This first murder was followed by 10 others that have been treated together as the Whitechapel murders. Five cases, numbers three to seven between 31 August and 9 November 1888, are regarded as most likely to have been the work of one man. All 11 cases involved female prostitutes as victims, all remain unsolved, and all occurred in and around the Whitechapel area. The summary chart illustrates some of the details:

Date and time	Victim	Location and circumstances	Injuries, and some of the examining doctor(s)
1 Tuesday 3 April 1888 1.30am	**Emma Elizabeth Smith** 45 years	Osborn Street, Whitechapel Assaulted with blunt instrument and robbed by 3 men	Ruptured peritoneum and abdominal organs Right ear torn Head injuries Dr George Haslip
2 Tuesday 7 August 1888 2am–3.30am	**Martha Tabram** (or Turner) 37 years	George Yard Buildings, George Yard, Whitechapel Stabbed 39 times, with some injuries thought to be caused by a dagger	Multiple stab wounds Dr Timothy Robert Killeen
3 Friday 31 August 1888 2.30am–3.45am	**Mary Ann Nichols** 45 years	Buck's Row, Whitechapel Slaughtermen and John Pizer suspected	Throat cut Disembowelled Dr Rees Ralph Llewellyn
4 Saturday 8 September 1888 1.45am–6.10am	**Annie Chapman** (or Siffey) 45 years	Rear Yard 29 Hanbury Street, Spitalfields Joseph Isenschmid suspected	Throat cut Disembowelled Dr George Bagster Phillips
5 Sunday 30 September 1888 12.45am–1am	**Elizabeth Stride** (or Watts or 'Long Liz') 37 years	Dutfield's Yard, by 40 Berner Street, Commercial Road East Murderer possibly disturbed in the act.	Throat cut Dr George Bagster Phillips Dr Frederick William Blackwell
6 Sunday 30 September 1888 1.35am–1.45am	**Catherine Eddowes** (or Kate Kelly) 43 years	Mitre Square, Aldgate, City of London Part of victim's blood-stained apron found in Goulston Street	Throat cut. Disembowelled Right ear cut through Uterus and left kidney removed. Dr Frederick Gordon Brown Dr George William Sequeira Dr William Sedgwick Saunders Dr George Bagster Phillips Dr Thomas Bond
7 Friday 9 November 1888 1am–10.45am	**Mary Jane Kelly** (or Marie Jeannette Kelly) 25 years	13 Miller's Court, 26 Dorset Street, Spitalfields Murder committed in victim's lodgings	Throat cut Disembowelled Numerous gashes and mutilations Heart removed Dr George Bagster Phillips Dr Frederick Gordon Brown Dr Thomas Bond Dr John R Gabe

Date and time	Victim	Location and circumstances	Injuries, and some of the examining doctor(s)
8 Thursday 20 December 1888	**Rose Mylett** (or Lizzie Davis)	Clarke's Yard, High Street, Poplar No signs of violence immediately apparent Victim seen arguing with two sailors	Strangled with cord Dr George Bagster Phillips Dr Matthew Brownfield Dr Charles Alfred Hebbert Dr Thomas Bond Dr Alexander MacKellar
9 Wednesday 17 July 1889 12.20am–12.50am	**Alice McKenzie** 39 years	Castle Alley, Whitechapel Dr Phillips concluded that the knife used was smaller than most of the other cases he had seen.	Throat cut Abdomen slashed Dr George Bagster Phillips Dr Alexander MacKellar Dr Thomas Bond Dr Frederick Gordon Brown
10 Tuesday 10 September 1889 Before 5.30am	**Unidentified female torso** About 35 years	Railway arch, Pinchin Street, near Backchurch Lane, Whitechapel Body placed there after death.	Head and legs missing Abdomen slashed Dr Charles Alfred Hebbert Dr Frederick Gordon Brown Dr George Bagster Phillips Dr Thomas Bond
11 Friday 13 February 1891 1.45am–2.15am	**Frances Coles** About 26 years	Swallow Gardens, Royal Mint Street, Whitechapel James Sadler, sailor, arrested and discharged	Throat cut twice. No other mutilation. Dr George Bagster Phillips

MARTHA TABRAM

Four months after the first case, on Tuesday, 7 August 1888, Martha Tabram (or Turner) was found murdered on the first floor landing of George Yard Buildings, George Yard, Whitechapel. She had been stabbed no fewer than 39 times. Dr Killeen said that more than one weapon might have been used, and that an injury to the chest bone was probably caused by a dagger. Edmund Reid, the local inspector who investigated the case, had also dealt with the case of Emma Smith.

The dead woman's colleague, Mary Connelly alias 'Pearly Poll', also a prostitute, went to Commercial Street police station two days later, and explained that she and Martha had been with two soldiers from 10pm until 11.45pm, until they had paired off. Pearly Poll said that she would recognize both soldiers again. There was also another useful witness, PC 226 H Barrett, who had spoken to a soldier outside George Yard at about 2am. The soldier had told the officer that he was waiting for his mate, who had gone away with a girl. Identification parades were arranged at the local barracks and PC Barrett picked out one man, but then changed his mind, later choosing a second soldier. Both soldiers were investigated and eliminated from suspicion. Pearly Poll herself picked out two soldiers, and said that she herself had been with one of them, whilst the other went off with Martha Tabram, but both men were eliminated from the inquiry. One had been with a woman, supposedly his wife, at an address in Hammersmith Road on the night in question; the other man had been recorded as returning to the barracks at 10.05pm. Because each soldier could prove an alibi, the case remained unsolved.

MARY ANN NICHOLS

Mary Ann Nichols was murdered just over three weeks later, on 31 August 1888, in Buck's Row, Whitechapel. At this point, the police began to think that all three murders might be linked. Nichols was also a prostitute and her clothing showed that she had lived at times in the Lambeth workhouse. She had been disembowelled and her throat deeply cut from left to right, as if by a left-handed person; it was this injury that was to mark out a definite link with later murders. There was no money in her pockets, and at 2.30am she had told another woman, in an eloquent testimony of the way people lived then, that she was trying to obtain four pence (2p) to pay for a bed in the lodging house.

A newspaper cutting from later in the day of 31 August reported:

> [police] officers engaged in the case are pushing their inquiries in the neighbourhood as to the doings of certain gangs known to frequent these parts, and an opinion is gaining ground amongst them that the murderers are the same who committed the two previous murders near the same spot. It is believed that these gangs, who make their appearance during the early hours of the morning, are in the habit of blackmailing these poor creatures, and where their demands are refused, violence follows. (HO 144/220/A49301B f179)

On 7 September, Inspector Helson, who was undertaking inquiries with Inspector Abberline from Scotland Yard, reported:

The inquiry has revealed the fact that a man named Jack Pizer, alias Leather Apron, has, for some considerable period been in the habit of ill-using prostitutes in this, and other parts of the Metropolis, and careful search has been, and is continued to be made to find this man in order that his movements may be accounted for on the night in question, although at present there is no evidence whatsoever against him.

MEPO 3/140 ff. 235–8

ANNIE CHAPMAN

The suspect, John (or Jack) Pizer, was found three days later, but not until after the fourth murder had occurred on Saturday 8 September. The day after Mary Nichols' funeral, Inspector Chandler was called to Hanbury Street, where Annie Chapman (alias Siffey) was found dead.

[There was] a woman lying on her back, dead, left arm resting on left breast, legs drawn up, abducted small intestines and flap of the abdomen lying on right side, above right shoulder attached by a cord with the rest of the intestines inside the body; two flaps of skin from the lower part of the abdomen lying in a large quantity of blood above the left shoulder; throat cut deeply from left and back in a jagged manner right round throat...
(MEPO 3/140 ff. 9–11)

This inquiry was also allocated to Inspector Abberline in view of the obvious similarities between the Mary Nichols and the Annie Chapman murders: their throats had been cut and they had suffered other similar injuries, they had been killed only eight days apart, in the same area of London, and in places used by prostitutes. Two brass rings missing from Annie Chapman's fingers were never recovered. A witness, Mrs Long, saw the back of a man who was talking to Annie Chapman at 5.30am. She thought he was wearing a brown deerstalker hat, a dark coat and might have been a foreigner. *The Times* of 20 September reported that she said he had the appearance of being shabby but genteel.

Dr Phillips, the Police Divisional Surgeon, believed the murder weapon to be a small amputating knife, or a well-ground butcher's knife, narrow and thin, with a blade six to eight inches long, used by somebody with anatomical knowledge. Some organs were missing, and the coroner informed the inquest jury that at least one medical school had been approached for similar female organs required in America. This was published in *The Times* of 27 September 1888 and became public knowledge.

The suspect John Pizer, or 'Leather Apron', was arrested two days after Annie Chapman's murder. Pizer's alibi for the night of Mary Nichols' murder was confirmed by a lodging house proprietor from Holloway Road. The prisoner also gave a corroborated account of where he had stayed on 8 September, the night of Annie Chapman's murder, despite being picked out in an identification parade by a man who said he had seen Pizer threatening a woman in Hanbury Street where Annie's body had been found. Pizer appeared at the inquest into Annie Chapman's death on 12 September and the next day it was reported in *The Times* that he said he 'had cleared his character'.

A mentally ill, unemployed butcher, Joseph Isenschmid, was also treated as a suspect. His wife said he was missing from home and that he carried large butcher's knives around with him, but when he was arrested, no blood was found on his clothing. He had, however, been seen with blood on his hands at 7am on the morning of Annie Chapman's murder. He was eventually confined to an asylum.

LETTERS TO THE POLICE

The first anonymous letter about the Whitechapel Murders was apparently received at Scotland Yard on 25 September 1888, and fuelled the theory that the murderer was a horse slaughterer:

> Dear Sir
>
> I do wish to give myself up. I am in misery with nightmare. I am the man who committed all these murders in the last six months. My name is [black coffin shape] and I am a horse slauterer and work at [name and address blacked out]. I have found the woman I wanted that is Chapman, and I done what I called slautered her but if any one comes I will surrender, but I am not going to walk to the station by myself so I am yours truly [black shape].

Keep the Boro' Road clear or I might take a trip up there.

[Photo of knife]

This is the knife that I done these murders with. It is a small handle with a large long blade, sharpe both sides.   MEPO 3/142 docket no 244, ff. 4–5

On the same day a more famous anonymous letter was written – the first to be signed off as 'Jack the Ripper'. It was received on 27 September by the Central News Agency, 5 New Bridge Street, Ludgate Circus, and has become known as the 'Dear Boss' letter (see plate 13). It was initially treated as a joke before being passed on to Scotland Yard two days later:

Dear Boss

I keep on hearing the police have caught me but they won't fix me just yet. I have laughed when they look so clever and talk about being on the right track. That joke about Leather Apron gave me real fits. I am down on whores and I shan't quit ripping them till I do get buckled. Grand work the last one was. I gave the lady no time to squeal. How can they catch me now. I love my work and want to start again. You will soon hear of me with my funny little games. I saved some of the proper red stuff in a ginger beer bottle over the last job to write with but it went thick like glue and I can't use it. Red ink is fit enough I hope ha ha. The next job I do I shall clip the lady's ears off and send to the police officers just for jolly wouldn't you. Keep this letter back till I do a bit more work, then give it out straight. My knife's so sharp I want to get to work right away if I get a chance. Good Luck.

Yours truly

Jack the Ripper

Don't mind me giving the trade name.

Wasn't good enough to post this before I got all the red ink off my hands curse it. No luck yet. They say I'm a doctor now ha ha.   MEPO 3/3153 ff. 1–4

Newspapers carried the story of the letter received from 'Jack the Ripper' on 1 October, together with news of a blood-stained postcard with similar handwriting, postmarked the same day, which had been sent to the Central News Agency (see plate 14).

I wasn't codding dear old Boss when I gave you the tip. You'll hear about saucy Jacky's work tomorrow. Double event this time. Number one squealed a bit, couldn't finish straight off. Had no time to get ears for police. Thanks for keeping last letter back till I got to work again.

Jack the Ripper   MEPO 3/142 ff. 2–3

These last two communications were reproduced on a police poster, dated 3 October, in a public appeal to try and trace the handwriting. The newspaper publicity and the reproduction of the letter and postcard generated enormous interest. But there was something very sinister about the postcard's wording: it used the phrase 'double event'. The day before the card's postmark, in the early hours of Sunday morning, 30 September, a 'double event' had indeed occurred: two more murders, of prostitutes Elizabeth Stride and Catherine Eddowes, were committed.

ELIZABETH STRIDE

It was at 1am when Louis Diemshitz, the secretary of a Socialist club, found the body of a woman in Dutfield's Yard in Berner Street, Commercial Road East. The woman had been killed very recently, and the murderer might well have been disturbed by the arrival of members of the club. Chief Inspector Donald Swanson reported that the body, later identified as Elizabeth Stride, was 'lying on left side, left arm extended from elbow, cachous lying in hand, right arm over stomach, back of hand & inner surface of wrist dotted with blood ... throat deeply gashed.'

PC 452 H. Smith had seen Elizabeth Stride, a prostitute, in Berner Street at 12.35am talking to a man whom he described as about 28 years of age, 5 foot 7 inches in height, with a dark complexion, a small black moustache, and dressed in a black coat with a white collar and tie. A witness, Israel Schwartz, saw a man molesting a woman who was screaming, and a second man lighting his pipe, to whom the first man called out 'Lipski'. The police interviewed and searched all the members present in the Socialist Club, and numerous inquiries were undertaken in the vicinity to try to trace the perpetrator. Elizabeth Stride's throat had also been cut, but there were few other injuries of significance. A tear in her left earlobe was an old injury that had already healed. The police searched the yard, but could find no trace of the weapon. The killer had left the scene, apparently still carrying his blood-stained knife.

A man and a woman had been seen standing together at the corner of Berner Street for some time, late that evening. Matthew Packer, a fruiterer who kept a shop at 44 Berner Street, thought that he recognized the body of Elizabeth Stride in the mortuary as the woman who had bought some grapes from his shop that evening; indeed, traces of grapes were found at the scene of the crime. At Scotland Yard, a number of sketches were prepared from descriptions of the man, and, in an early forerunner of Identikit, they were then shown to Matthew Packer, who picked out the one that best corresponded with his memory. He was also shown a number of photographs of criminals. The *Daily Telegraph* recounted these developments in their edition of 6 October, including the sketch selected by Matthew Packer. These developments led to the detention of a suspect, John Langan in France, but he was eliminated from inquiries.

CATHERINE EDDOWES

The second murder in the early hours of 30 September was in Mitre Square, Aldgate, within the jurisdiction of the City of London Police. Catherine Eddowes was found murdered and disembowelled at 1.45am. Her uterus and left kidney were missing, and her right ear had been cut through. Police officers found part of the dead woman's blood-stained apron a few streets away in Goulston Street on Metropolitan Police territory. A message was found on the wall above it, written in chalk: 'The Jewes are the men that will not be blamed for nothing.' Inspector McWilliam of the City Police ordered the writing to be photographed, but Sir Charles Warren, the Commissioner at Scotland Yard (see plate 16), had it erased before the photographer arrived because of its anti-Semitic nature. Chief Inspector Swanson reported that police officers who had seen the writing said that it bore no resemblance to that featured in the 'Dear Boss' letter, but Warren's actions endeared himself neither to the City of London investigators nor to the high levels in the Home Office.

The police task of understanding the possible linkage between the murders had now become more complicated by the responsibility of the City of London

Police for the Catherine Eddowes case. A witness, Joseph Lawende (or Lewin), who had seen Catherine Eddowes shortly before her murder, described the man who was with her as about 30 years of age, about 5 foot 7 inches in height, with a fair complexion and the appearance of a sailor. A chart, based on some of the information contained in Swanson's report to the Home Office of 19 September and forming the basis for a notice in the *Police Gazette* of 19 October, shows the various descriptions of suspects for three of the murders:

Comparison of the descriptions given of the men who were observed near the scene at the time of the several murders

	Annie Chapman		**Elizabeth Stride**		**Eddowes**
	Description of man seen by Mrs Long at 5.30	[ ] man seen at 12.35 by police constable	First man seen by Schwartz with woman at 12.45	Man seen on the opposite side of the street by Schwartz	Man seen with woman at 1.35
Age	40	28	30	35	30
Height	–	5' 7"	5' 5"	5' 11"	5' 7 or 8"
Complexion	–	dark	fair	fresh	–
Hair	–	–	dark	light brown	–
Moustache	–	small, dark	small brown	brown	fair
Face	–	–	full	–	–
Figure	–	–	broad shouldered	–	medium build
Coat	vy. dark	black, diagonal	dark jacket	dark with overcoat	pepper and salt colour; loose jacket
Trousers	–	–	dark	–	–
Hat	–	Hard felt	black cap with peak	old black hat; hard felt; wide brim	Grey cloth cap with peak of same colour
Collar	–	white collar and tie	–	–	–
Remarks	Looked like a foreigner	–	–	Clay pipe in his mouth	Reddish handkerchief tied in a knot round his neck: looked like a sailor

MEPO 3/2890

Yet even as the police were attempting to integrate any evidence common to those murders, the goading letters continued. On 16 October, Mr Lusk, Chairman of the East End Vigilance Committee formed as a result of the murders, received half a human kidney through the post, with another anonymous letter, signed off as 'catch me when you can Mishter Lusk' and in different handwriting from the 'Dear Boss' letter. The human kidney was the one aspect that distinguished this communication from the many letters and postcards signed 'Jack the Ripper' that had started to arrive in alarming numbers. Many of these letters were sent in the month of October, but mercifully no Whitechapel murders occurred that month. October saw the Commissioner, Sir Charles Warren, being pursued across Hyde Park in a personal experiment to test the efficiency of bloodhounds, as well as the arrests of a number of suspects, all of whom were cleared.

MARY JANE KELLY

After a period of five weeks, on Friday, 9 November 1888, the seventh murder occurred. The tension over whether another incident might occur is reflected in the promptness with which Commissioner Sir Charles Warren, under considerable pressure after erasing the writing on the wall in Goulston Street, sent a telegram to the Home Office (see plate 15):

> Sir Charles Warren to Mr Lushington [Permanent Under Secretary at Home Office]
>
> Mutilated dead body of woman reported to be found this morning inside room of house in Dorset Street Spitalfields.
> Information just received.
> 9.11.88   HO 144/221/A49301F

The latest victim turned out to be Mary Jane Kelly, inevitably an 'unfortunate', a euphemism for a prostitute, who had been found dead inside her room at 13 Miller's Court, Dorset Street, Spitalfields. Thomas Bowyer, who had called at 10.45am to collect the rent on behalf of his employer, found the body. Mary Cox, another 'unfortunate' who lived at the same address, had seen the latest victim returning to her room with a man at about 11.45pm. She gave evidence at the inquest:

As they were going into her room I said 'Good night Mary Jane'. She was very drunk and could scarcely answer me, but said 'Good night'. The man was carrying a quart can of beer. I shortly afterwards heard her singing. I went out shortly after twelve and returned about one o'clock and she was still singing in her room. I went out again shortly after one o'clock and returned at 3 o'clock , there was no light in her room and all was quiet, and I heard no noise all night.

(MJ/SPC, NE1888 Box 3, Case Paper 19, London Metropolitan Archives)

Mary Jane Kelly had been murdered in her ground floor room. Her throat was cut and she had been terribly mutilated. Police inquiries were made, but with no more success than the other cases.

Dr Thomas Bond, the police surgeon for A Division, conducted a post mortem examination on Mary Jane Kelly. His report was probably the first medical analysis linking murders together on medical evidence:

I beg to report that I have read the notes of the 4 Whitechapel Murders, viz:

1. Buck's Row
2. Hanbury Street
3. Berner's Street
4. Mitre Square

I have also made a post-mortem examination of the mutilated remains of a woman found yesterday in a small room in Dorset Street.

1 All five murders were no doubt committed by the same hand. In the first four, the throats appear to have been cut from left to right. In the last case, owing to the extensive mutilation, it is impossible to say in what direction the fatal cut was made, but arterial blood was found on the wall in splashes close to where the woman's head must have been lying.

2 All the circumstances surrounding the murders lead me to form the opinion that the women must have been lying down when murdered and in every case the throat was first cut.

3 In the four murders of which I have seen the notes only, I cannot

form a very definite opinion as to the time that had elapsed between the murder and the discovering of the body...

4 In all the cases there appears to be no evidence of struggling and the attacks were probably so sudden and made in such a position that the women could neither resist nor cry out. In the Dorset Street case, the corner of the sheet to the right of the woman's head was much cut and saturated with blood, indicating that the face may have been covered with the sheet at the time of the attack.

5 In the four first cases, the murderer must have attacked from the right side of the victim. In the Dorset Street case, he must have attacked from in front or from the left, as there would be no room for him between the wall and the part of the bed on which the woman was lying. Again, the blood had flowed down on the right side of the woman and spurted on to the wall.

6 The murderer would not necessarily be splashed or deluged with blood, but his hands and arms must have been covered and parts of his clothing must certainly have been smeared with blood.

7 The mutilations in each case, excepting the Berner's Street one, were all of the same character and shewed clearly that in all the murders, the object was mutilation.

8 In each case the mutilation was inflicted by a person who had no scientific nor anatomical knowledge. In my opinion he does not even possess the technical knowledge of a butcher or horse slaughterer or any person accustomed to cut up dead animals.

9 The instrument must have been a strong knife at least six inches long, very sharp, pointed at the top and about an inch in width. It may have been a clasp knife, a butcher's knife or a surgeon's knife. I think it was no doubt a straight knife.

10 The murderer must have been a man of physical strength and of great coolness and daring. There is no evidence that he had an accomplice. He must in my opinion be a man subject to periodical attacks of Homicidal and erotic mania. The character of the mutilations indicate that the man may be in a condition sexually, that may be called

satyriasis. It is of course possible that the Homicidal impulse may have developed from a revengeful or brooding condition of the mind, or that Religious Mania may have been the original disease, but I do not think either hypothesis is likely. The murderer in external appearance is quite likely to be a quiet, inoffensive looking man, probably middle-aged and neatly and respectably dressed. I think he must be in the habit of wearing a cloak or overcoat, or he could hardly have escaped notice in the streets if the blood on his hands or clothes were visible.

11   Assuming the murderer to be such a person as I have just described, he would probably be solitary and eccentric in his habits, also he is most likely to be a man without regular occupation, but with some small income or pension. He is possibly living among respectable persons who have some knowledge of his character and habits, and who may have grounds for suspicion that he is not quite right in his mind at times. Such persons would probably be unwilling to communicate suspicions to the Police for fear of trouble or notoriety, whereas if there were a prospect of reward it might overcome their scruples.

HO 144/221/A49301C ff. 220–3

The resignation of Commissioner Sir Charles Warren was announced on the day of Mary Kelly's murder. There is no evidence to suggest that Mary Kelly's murder itself was the cause of his resignation; he had been criticized for publishing an inappropriate article on 'The Policing of London' in *Murray's Magazine* and relationships between the Home Office and the Commissioner left a lot to be desired during this period. His successor was James Monro, with whom Warren had a major disagreement concerning the appointment of Melville Macnaghten to a senior post in the Criminal Investigation Department. Despite the changes at the top of Scotland Yard, the investigation into Mary Kelly's death was no more successful than the others had been.

ROSE MYLETT

The new Commissioner, who was to serve for only a little over 18 months, made an understandable personal commitment to brief the Home Secretary at length when another prostitute, Rose Mylett, was found dead in Poplar,

25. Sept. 1888.

Dear Boss

I keep on hearing the police have caught me. but they wont fix me just yet. I have laughed when they look so clever and talk about being on the right track. That joke about Leather apron gave me real fits. I am down on whores and I shant quit ripping them till I do get buckled. Grand work the last job was. I gave the lady no time to squeal How can they catch me now. I love my work and want to start again. You will soon hear of me with my funny little games. I saved some of the proper red stuff in a ginger beer bottle over the last job to write with but it went thick like glue and I cant use it. Red ink is fit enough I hope ha. ha. The next job I do I shall clip the ladys ears off and send to the

police officers just for jolly wouldnt you. Keep this letter back till I do a bit more work. then give it out straight My knife's so nice and sharp I want to get to work right away if I get a chance. Good luck.

yours truly
Jack the Ripper

Dont mind one giving the trade name

(sideways text) wasnt good enough to post this before I got all the red ink off my hands curse it No luck yet. They say I'm a doctor now ha ha

POST CARD

THE ADDRESS ONLY TO BE WRITTEN ON THIS SIDE

LONDON OC 1 88

Central News Office
London City
E.C

3

OFFICE

I wasnt codding dear old Boss when I gave you the tip, you'll hear about saucy Jacky's work tomorrow double event this time number one squealed a bit couldnt finish straight off. had not time to get ears for police thanks for keeping last letter back till I got to work again. Jack the Ripper

13 ABOVE The 'Dear Boss' letter, the first to be received by Scotland Yard signed 'Jack the Ripper' (MEPO 3/3153).

14 BELOW Stained postcard signed 'Jack the Ripper' referring to a 'double event' when two murders occurred in the early hours of Sunday 30 September 1888 (MEPO 3/142).

15 BELOW Telegram from Commissioner Sir Charles Warren on the day his resignation was announced, informing the Home Secretary of the seventh Whitechapel murder (Mary Kelly) (HO 144/221/ A49301).

16 RIGHT Rare picture of Sir Charles Warren, Commissioner 1886–8 (COPY 1/443).

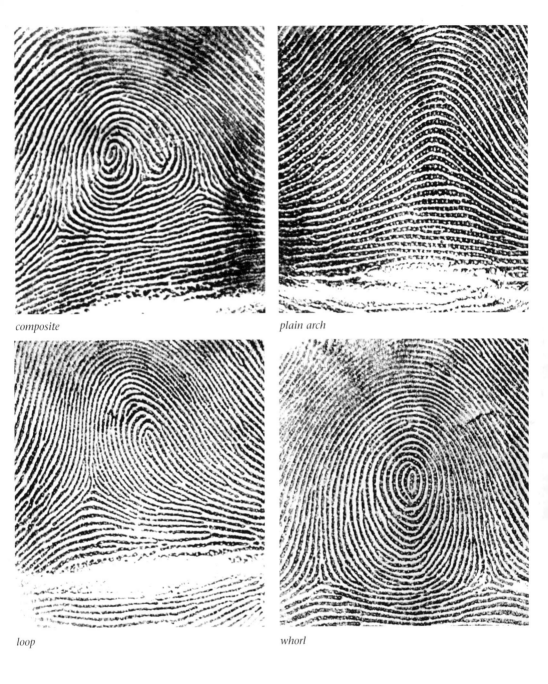

composite

plain arch

loop

whorl

17 The main fingerprint patterns from which Edward Henry was able to design his classification and retrieval system for fingerprint collections.

Nº	Storage	Divn:	Description of Article	Date Received	From whom received
1 FP194		P	On window frame Door Knob	1904	Insp Morgan Partick FP.194 Murder
2		V	Do		
3			Lantern		C C Windsor

ALFRED STRATTON   ALBERT STRATTON

OLD BAILEY
5·MAY·05

18 TOP Exhibit register of the Fingerprint Bureau showing the entry for Harry Jackson, the first person convicted on fingerprint evidence in Britain. An added note appears to indicate the examination of a door knob, perhaps in connection with the apparently unsolved 1904 Scottish murder of Lucy McArthur at Whiteinch, near Partick.

19 ABOVE 1905 court sketch of Alfred and Albert Stratton, the first men to be convicted of murder in Britain on fingerprint evidence.

20 RIGHT Detective Chief Superintendent Frederick Cherrill, a distinguished Head of the Fingerprint Branch 1938–53 (MEPO 13/190).

Address where Offence Committed	Offence	Result & Remarks
Denmark Hill	Burglary C.C.Ct. 2.9.02	Hy Jackson, 2947.00. at Sentenced to 7 years P.S.
...ston House Wimbledon	Burglary Kingston	Wm Hall, 3318.99 at Assizes. 25.8.03 5 Yrs P.S.
—	Burglary	Thos Wilson 630.98. at Reading

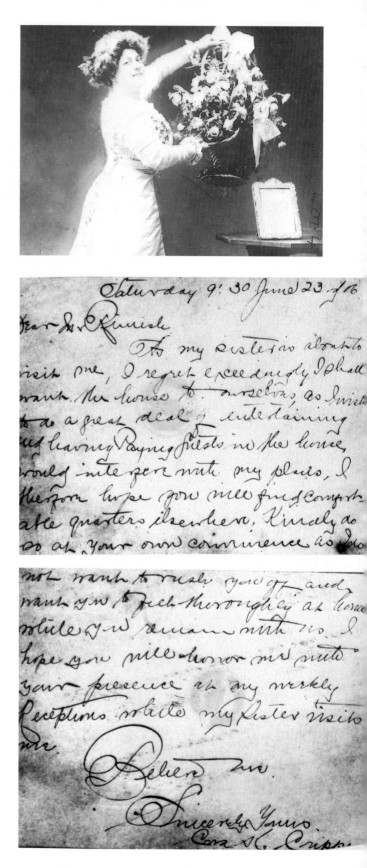

21 A studio portrait of Cora Crippen and a sample of her handwriting in a letter to a former lodger at 39 Hilldrop Crescent (MEPO 3/198).

Saturday 9: 30 June 23 /16

Dear Mr Kunish

As my sister is about to visit me, I regret exceedingly I shall want the house to ourselves, as I wish to do a great deal of entertaining and having paying guests in the house, would interfere with my plans, I therefore hope you will find comfortable quarters elsewhere, Kindly do so at your own convenience as I do not want to rush you off, and want you to feel thoroughly at home while you remain with us. I hope you will honor me with your presence at my weekly receptions while my sister visits me.

Believe me.

Sincerely Yours,
Cora K. Crippen

22 ABOVE Police officers in the garden of 39 Hilldrop Crescent, which was searched for Cora Crippen's remains: Walter Dew is on the right; and LEFT the cellar in which human flesh was found (MEPO 3/198).

METROPOLITAN POLICE

MURDER
AND MUTILATION.

Portraits, Description and Specimen of Handwriting of HAWLEY HARVEY CRIPPEN, alias Peter Crippen, alias Franckel; and ETHEL CLARA LE NEVE, alias Mrs. Crippen, and Neave.

Wanted for the Murder of CORA CRIPPEN, otherwise Belle Elmore; Kunigunde Mackamotzki; Marsangar and Turner, on, or about, 2nd February last.

Description of Crippen.—Age 50, height 5 ft. 3 or 4, complexion fresh, hair light brown, inclined sandy, scanty, bald on top, rather long scanty moustache, somewhat straggly, eyes grey, bridge of nose rather flat, false teeth, medium build, throws his feet outwards when walking. May be clean shaven or wearing a beard and gold rimmed spectacles, and may possibly assume a wig.

Sometimes wears a jacket suit, and at other times frock coat and silk hat. May be dressed in a brown jacket suit, brown hat and stand up collar (size 15).

Somewhat slovenly appearance, wears his hat rather at back of head

Very plausible and quiet spoken, remarkably cool and collected demeanour.

Speaks French and probably German. Carries Firearms.

An American citizen, and by profession a Doctor.

Has lived in New York, Philadelphia, St. Louis, Detroit, Michigan, Coldwater, and other parts of America.

May obtain a position as assistant to a doctor or eye specialist, or may practise as an eye specialist, Dentist, or open a business for the treatment of deafness, advertising freely.

Has represented Munyon's Remedies, in various cities in America.

Description of Le Neve alias Neave.—A shorthand writer and typist, age 27, height 5 ft. 5, complexion pale, hair light brown (may dye same), large grey or blue eyes, good teeth, nice looking, rather long straight nose (good shape), medium build, pleasant, lady-like appearance. Quiet, subdued manner, talks quietly, looks intently when in conversation. A native of London.

Dresses well, but quietly, and may wear a blue serge costume (coat reaching to hips) trimmed heavy braid, about ¼ inch wide, round edge, over shoulders and pockets. Three large braid buttons down front, about size of a florin, three small ones on each pocket, two on each cuff, several rows of stitching round bottom of skirt; or a light grey shadow-stripe costume, same style as above, but trimmed grey moire silk instead of braid, and two rows of silk round bottom of skirt; or a white princess robe with gold sequins; or a mole coloured striped costume with black moire silk collar; or a dark vieuxrose cloth costume, trimmed black velvet collar; or a light heliotrope dress.

May have in her possession and endeavour to dispose of same:—a round gold brooch, with points radiating zig-zag from centre, each point about an inch long, diamond in centre, each point set brilliants, the brooch in all being slightly larger than a half-crown; and two single stone diamond rings, and a diamond and sapphire (or ruby) ring, stones rather large.

Absconded 9th inst. and may have left, or will endeavour to leave the country.

Please cause every enquiry at Shipping Offices, Hotels, and other likely places, and cause ships to be watched.

Information to be given to the Metropolitan Police Office, New Scotland Yard, London. S.W., or at any Police Station.

E. R. HENRY,
The Commissioner of Police of the Metropolis.

Metropolitan Police Office,
New Scotland Yard. 16th July, 1910.

23 Wanted poster published during the hunt for
Dr Crippen and Ethel le Neve (MEPO 3/198).

early in the morning of 20 December 1888. There were no signs of violence or a struggle. She had been strangled with a moderately thick cord, and one of her earrings was missing. There were, therefore, significant differences between the attack on her and the five murders between the end of August and November that year.

ALICE MCKENZIE

The murder of Alice McKenzie in Castle Alley, Whitechapel, on 17 July 1889 seemed more likely to be linked to the series of killings, because her throat was cut and her abdomen also bore knife wounds. Dr Bond performed the second post mortem examination, and stated in his report:

> The wounds on the abdomen could have nothing to do with the cause of death & were in my opinion inflicted after death. I see in this murder evidence of similar design to the former Whitechapel murders viz. sudden onslaught on the prostrate woman, the throat skilfully and resolutely cut, with subsequent mutilation, each mutilation indicating sexual thoughts & a desire to mutilate the abdomen and sexual organs.
>
> I am of the opinion that the murder was performed by the same person who committed the former series of Whitechapel murders.
>
> MEPO 3/140 ff. 259–62

This medical opinion was challenged by Dr Phillips, who had personally examined other Whitechapel murder victims. He believed that the difference in the abdominal wounds was significant, and thought that it was not certain that the same man had been involved.

THE PINCHIN STREET TORSO

It was not entirely clear as to when the series of murders had begun, and there were similar issues about when they came to an end. Three months after the murder of Alice McKenzie, on 10 September 1889, the remains of an unidentified female torso were discovered under a railway arch in Pinchin Street, Whitechapel. Chief Inspector Donald Swanson was clear that this tenth murder was not part of the main series, explaining in his report that:

1st Upon the spot where the trunk was found, there was no evidence of any blood, and a foot mark from the nature of the ground was an impossibility; nor was there left anything in the shape of a cloth or sack to carry the trunk in.

2nd The place of disposal must have been a selected spot; i.e. it must have been selected by viewing, for on all sides of it not a single inhabitant resides … disposal was easy.

3rd The appearance of the trunk, minus head and legs, was as follows … but the dismemberment had taken place at an earlier period than the head … there is absolutely nothing by which the trunk could be identified.

…death could not have taken place by cutting the throat…What becomes apparent is the absence of the attack … as in the series of Whitechapel murders beginning at Bucks Row and ending in Miller's Court. Certainly if there was time enough for the murderer to cut off the head and limbs, there was time enough to mutilate as in the series mentioned. It appears to go side by side with the Rainham, Whitehall and Chelsea murders. MEPO 3/142 ff. 2–3

Swanson's final comments about the other cases refer to three unsolved murders, none of which was in Whitechapel and which were also puzzling the police. One case, known as the Whitehall Mystery, was the torso of a woman found in the cellars of the new building that would soon be the headquarters of the Metropolitan Police at New Scotland Yard.

FRANCES COLES

Seventeen months later, the eleventh and final victim, prostitute Frances Coles, was found dead at 2.15am on the morning of Friday 13 February 1891 in Swallow Gardens, Whitechapel. PC 240H Thompson found the murdered woman lying in the road with her throat cut. The body was not mutilated in any other way, and Dr Phillips believed that the nature of the wound and the posture of the body also suggested that the case was not the work of the man who had perpetrated any of the other Whitechapel murders.

Energetic inquiries were again made, but this time arguably with better effect. Sergeant John Don arrested a man called James Sadler, who admitted having consorted with Frances Coles on more than one occasion. As a sailor, he could have been implicated in the murder of Catherine Eddowes, but the eye-witness in Mitre Square could not identify him. The belief that police had at last arrested 'Jack the Ripper' gained ground, and he was charged with murdering Frances Coles.

Numerous inquiries were made into Sadler's background and the dates of his employment and discharge on various ships plying to and from the London docks, but after a period in custody, he was released on 3 March by the magistrates at Thames police court when the prosecuting advocate offered no evidence against him. The incident did not help Sadler's already unhappy marriage, and later, on 16 May 1892, at Lambeth magistrates court, he was bound over to keep the peace after his wife had complained that Sadler had threatened to cut her throat.

The murder of Frances Coles remained unsolved, and it was the last of the deaths that could be classified as a Whitechapel murder. Scotland Yard, now under the leadership of yet another new Commissioner, Sir Edward Bradford, started to recover from a period of unprecedented public criticism for their failure to solve so many murders.

WHO WROTE THE LETTERS?

Many modern researchers have pored over the details of who was responsible for the Whitechapel Murders, and whether the murderer did in fact write the important 'Jack the Ripper' letters. It is clear that the writer of the postcard, dated 1 October, knew of the 'double event' at a very early stage, and, if not the murderer, the writer was privy to some very early information as well as the contents of the 'Dear Boss' letter. There was speculation, even soon afterwards, that the postcard and the 'Dear Boss' letter were part of a hoax from a member of the press. Chief Inspector Littlechild wrote, in retirement, that officers at Scotland Yard had suspected Tom Bulling of the Central News Agency, or his chief, Mr Moore.

THE MACNAGHTEN MEMORANDUM

The earliest surviving official analysis of the murders is an 1894 report by Sir Melville Macnaghten, then second-in-command to Dr Robert Anderson, Head of the CID. It was prompted by a series of reports in the *Sun* newspaper (13–19 February 1894) that a man called Thomas Cutbush, who had been detained for stabbing women in Kennington, was the Whitechapel murderer. A second version of the memorandum, known as the Aberconway version, survived through Melville Macnaghten's family. A third, but now missing version is known as the Donner version.

Macnaghten, who did not take up his post until June 1889, by which time the most frequently acknowledged cases in the series had already occurred, put forward three suspects as examples of men who were more likely than Cutbush to have committed the Whitechapel Murders. There was another dimension to this case for Scotland Yard because Thomas Cutbush, who was convicted in April 1891, was the nephew of Superintendent Charles Cutbush who resigned, suffering from general debility, in August 1891 and later committed suicide. *The Sun* newspaper did not mention Cutbush by name.

Macnaghten was said to have had an astonishing memory for criminals and their crimes, but modern researchers have drawn attention to apparent factual errors, or inconsistency with other reports, about, for instance, the details of the suspect Druitt, the eye-witnesses who had apparently seen the murderer, and the Pinchin Street torso. Nevertheless, the document on the Scotland Yard file does appear to represent Macnaghten's opinion on the case:

> The case referred to in the sensational story told in 'the Sun' in its issue of 13th. Inst., & following dates, is that of Thomas Cutbush, who was arraigned at the London County Sessions in April 1891, on a charge of maliciously wounding Florence Grace Johnson, & attempting to wound Isabella Fraser Anderson in Kennington. He was found to be insane, and sentenced to be detained during Her Majesty's pleasure.
>
> This Cutbush, who lived with his mother and aunt at 14 Albert St. Kennington, escaped from the Lambeth Infirmary, (after he had been detained there only a few hours, as a lunatic) at noon on 5th. March 1891... The knife found on him was bought in Houndsditch about a

week before he was detained in the Infirmary. Cutbush was a nephew of the late Supt Executive.

Now the Whitechapel murderer had 5 victims – & 5 victims only, – his murders were:

(i) 31st. Aug '88. Mary Ann Nichols, at Buck's Row, who was found with her throat cut, & with (slight) stomach mutilation.

(ii) 8th. Sept '88. Annie Chapman – Hanbury St. Throat cut, stomach & private parts badly mutilated & some of the entrails placed round the neck.

(iii) 30th. Sept '88. Elizabeth Stride, Berner's [sic] street, throat cut, but nothing in shape of mutilation attempted, & on same date

(iv) Catherine Eddowes. Mitre Square, throat cut, & very bad mutilation, both of face & stomach.

(v) 9th November. Mary Jane Kelly. Miller's Court throat cut, and the whole of the body mutilated in the most ghastly manner.

The last murder is the only one that took place in a room, and the murderer must have been at least 2 hours engaged. A photo was taken of the woman, as she was found lying on the bed, without seeing which it is impossible to imagine the awful mutilation.

With regard to the double murder which took place on 30th. Sept, there is no doubt but that the man was disturbed by some Jews who drove up to a club, (close to which the body of Elizabeth Stride was found) and that he then, 'nondum satiatus', went in search of a further victim whom he found at Mitre Square ...

No one ever saw the Whitechapel murderer, many homicidal maniacs were suspected, but no shadow of proof could be thrown on any one. I may mention the cases of 3 men, any one of whom would have been more likely than Cutbush to have committed this series of murders:

(1) A Mr. M.J. Druitt, said to be a doctor & of good family, who disappeared at the time of the Miller's Court murder, & whose body (which was said to have been upwards of a month in the water) was found in the Thames on 31st. Decr., or about 7 weeks after that murder. He was sexually insane and from private inf. I have little doubt but that his own family believed him to have been the murderer.

(2) Kosminski, a Polish Jew, & resident in Whitechapel. This man became insane owing to many years indulgence in solitary vices. He had a great hatred of women, specially of the prostitute class, & had strong homicidal tendencies; he was removed to a lunatic asylum about March 1889. There were many circs. connected with this man which made him a strong 'suspect'.

(3) Michael Ostrog, a Russian doctor, and a convict, who was subsequently detained in a lunatic asylum as a homicidal maniac. The man's antecedents were of the worst possible type, and his whereabouts at the time of the murders could never be ascertained.

In the issue of 15th inst. it is said that a light overcoat was among the things found in Cutbush's house, and that a man in a light overcoat was seen talking to a woman in Backchurch Lane whose body with arms attached was found in Pinchin St. This is hopelessly incorrect! On 10th. Sept. '89 the naked body, with arms, of a woman was found wrapped in some sacking under a Railway arch in Pinchin St: the head & legs were never found nor was the woman ever identified. She had been killed at least 24 hours before the remains, (which had seemingly been brought from a distance), were discovered. The stomach was split up by a cut, and the head and legs had been severed in a manner identical with that of the woman whose remains were discovered in the Thames, in Battersea Park, & on the Chelsea Embankment on 4th June of the same year; and these murders had no connection whatever with the Whitechapel horrors. The Rainham mystery in 1887, & the Whitehall mystery (where portions of a woman's body were found under what is now New Scotland Yard) in 1888 were of a similar type to the Thames & Pinchin St crimes.

The theory that the Whitechapel murderer was left handed, or, at any rate, 'ambidexter' had its origins in the remark made by a doctor who examined the corpse of one of the earliest victims; other doctors did not agree with him.

With regard to the 4 additional murders ascribed by the writer in the Sun to the Whitechapel fiend:

(1) The body of Martha Tabram, a prostitute, was found on a common stair case in George Yard buildings on 7th. August 1888, the body had been repeatedly pierced, probably with a bayonet. This woman had, with a fellow prostitute, been in company of 2 soldiers in the early part of the evening; these men were arrested, but the second prostitute failed, or refused, to identify, and the soldiers were accordingly discharged.

(2) Alice McKenzie was found with her throat cut (or rather stabbed) in Castle Alley on 17th July 1889; no evidence was forthcoming and no arrests were made in connection with this case. The stab in the throat was of the same nature as in the case of the number

(3) Frances Coles, in Swallow Gardens, on 13th. February 1891, for which Thomas Sadler, a fireman, was arrested, &, after several remands, discharged. It was ascertained at the time that Sadler had sailed for the Baltic on 19th. July '89 & was in Whitechapel on the night of 17th. idem. He was a man of ungovernable temper & entirely addicted to drink, & the company of the lowest prostitutes.

(4) The case of the unidentified woman whose trunk was found in Pinchin St: on 10th. Sept. 1889 which has already been dealt with.

MEPO 3/140 ff. 177–83

There is apparently no other file reference to investigations into Macnaghten's three suspects, Druitt, Kosminski and Ostrog. There were, indeed, many arrests and suspects at the time for the Whitechapel Murders, but the relevant files are now missing.

THE LITTLECHILD, ANDERSON AND ABBERLINE THEORIES

Chief Inspector John George Littlechild, Head of the Special Branch from 1883 to 1893, wrote to a journalist in 1913 about Dr Tumblety (also known as Twomblety), a sexual offender with some antagonism towards women, who fled the country to Boulogne, after being bailed from Marlborough Street magistrates court in connection with a relatively minor case of gross indecency. His arrest took place on 7 November 1888, two days before the Mary Kelly murder, and he could feasibly have committed that offence whilst on bail, but there is no other evidence known against him.

Dr Robert Anderson was interviewed for *Windsor Magazine* and was quoted as strongly suspecting three men, who were not named, but who corresponded to Macnaghten's three suspects. From further interviews, it could be inferred that his strongest suspect was Kosminski. In Chief Inspector Swanson's personal copy of Robert Anderson's book, *The Lighter Side of My Official Life,* a note, apparently pencilled by Swanson, confirmed Kosminski as the suspect, stating that the man had been taken to Stepney workhouse and then to Colney Hatch, where he died shortly afterwards.

Chief Inspector Frederick Abberline was interviewed in March 1903, whilst in retirement, by *Pall Mall Gazette,* after the prosecution and death sentence passed on George Chapman, alias Severin Klosowski, for poisoning, in 1897, 1901 and 1902, three 'wives' who had assisted him in running a barber's shop and two public houses. Chapman had been apprenticed to a surgeon in Poland before he arrived in England some time after February 1887. Chapman had apparently lived in Cable Street at the time of most of the murders, but in 1890 moved to the corner of George Yard and Whitechapel High Street, close by where Martha Tabram had been killed in August 1888. He liked to wear a sailor's cap.

Some time after April 1891, Chapman went to New York and opened a barber's shop in Jersey City, but returned in about March 1892 separately from his wife, Lucy who had left him because of his violence towards her. It is said that there were a number of murders in America at about this time which were apparently similar to the Whitechapel series, but no records of these are known, apart from the murder of prostitute Carrie Brown, known as 'Old Shakespeare', in New York on the night of 23 April 1891. She suffered abdominal mutilation. The occupant of a neighbouring room in the hotel was convicted of the murder, but 11 years later, he was released after an appeal. Abberline is supposed to have said to Inspector George Godley, who had arrested Chapman, 'I see you have got Jack the Ripper at last'. Abberline therefore considered Chapman a suspect, but only after he had retired.

There was nothing other than circumstantial evidence against any of these men, but the modern police service would probably have been able to have confirmed or disproved their involvement by DNA or other forensic science tests which were unavailable to their nineteenth-century counterparts.

The pressure and speed of events, especially around the last weekend of September 1888, and the publicity surrounding the 'Jack the Ripper' letters would have stretched any police force. There was relatively little eye-witness evidence in the narrow streets and dark alleys of Whitechapel. Although extra police patrols were organized, they were unable to produce blanket coverage of every street and secluded yard where prostitutes might meet their clients.

The Whitechapel Murders remain a vivid testimony not only to the lurid fascination with sexually motivated attacks that inspire such taunting letters from disturbed and irresponsible characters, but also to the social and living conditions of the 'unfortunates' in that part of Victorian London.

THE 'YORKSHIRE RIPPER' HOAX

The effect of these murders has also been felt in modern times. The West Yorkshire police investigating the 'Yorkshire Ripper' murders, committed by Peter Sutcliffe between 1975 and 1981, received many hoax and taunting letters, some of which bore a striking resemblance to those received by Scotland Yard a century before. On 21 March 2006, John Humble, a 50-year-old unemployed labourer who had become obsessive about details of the Whitechapel murders and 'Jack the Ripper', was sentenced to eight years' imprisonment at Leeds Crown Court. He had sent the police an audiotape that had significantly diverted the attention of the West Yorkshire murder inquiry, and apparently contributed to Peter Sutcliffe being wrongly eliminated before he was eventually caught. Three murders in the series occurred between the date of Humble's hoax and the eventual arrest of Peter Sutcliffe, fuelling arguments that without Humble's actions, those deaths might have been prevented. Humble's hoax tape contained many details about the murders, but it eventually transpired that all the details in the letters and the tape had been mentioned in newspapers. Conversely, one of Sutcliffe's murders that had taken place in Bradford before Humble's tape was made was not mentioned on the tape. In hindsight, Humble's Wearside accent, identified at the time as from the Castletown area of Sunderland, should not have been used to eliminate suspects arising in the vast and complex inquiry into the murders committed by Peter Sutcliffe. Once publicized, the tape, like the letters in Whitechapel a century before, generated enormous public interest and reactions that required some form of police response, regardless of how useful they might be in pointing to the real killer.

The police were eventually able to identify John Humble as the author of the tape due to recent advances in DNA technology that enabled forensic scientists to determine the genetic details of the person who had licked and sealed an envelope used for the hoax. Humble's DNA had been added to the database after he had been cautioned for a minor incident many years after his actions had distorted the inquiry into the Peter Sutcliffe murders. The dramatic potential of the DNA database was again demonstrated. If that technology had been available in 1888, or even 90 years later in West Yorkshire, there would have been a far better chance of clarifying that crucial issue: was the author of the letter or tape, however plausible, the same person who had committed any of the murders?

CHAPTER SEVEN

Fingerprint evidence: finding the right match

Once a suspect had been identified and brought to court, the police had another problem: how to find out whether he had been in trouble before, perhaps under a different name? In settled communities, where people all knew each other, there was no real problem, but Victorian London was no such place. In 1878, Howard Vincent, Scotland Yard's Director of Criminal Intelligence, introduced a system of police officers visiting Newgate and Clerkenwell prisons to see if they could recognize any of the inmates who might have given false names. This was a good test for the police officers putting names to faces, but unless the prisoner admitted his identity, the whole process relied upon human memory. And human memory was fallible, as illustrated by the Adolf Beck case. So there was a great interest, in Britain and abroad, in developing a scientific approach that could guarantee the reliable identification of criminals and linkage with their record. In 1880, in France, for instance, Alphonse Bertillon invented a method of systematically measuring parts of the prisoner's body, a process that became known as *bertillonage*.

Fourteen years later, in 1894, Scotland Yard implemented a version of Bertillon's system using the name *anthropometry* (Greek for 'the measurement of man'). The system used five of Bertillon's criteria of measuring bones, but added two other identification features: the colour of the eyes – and fingerprints. Anthropometry lasted for a few years, but was effective only if one

The development of fingerprint analysis

The unique characteristics of fingerprints begin to form when the baby is a 6-month-old embryo in the womb. The development of scientific knowledge about fingerprints began with an Italian anatomist, Marcello Malpighi (1628–1694), who described the patterns on our fingertips as being part of the overall structure of the skin. A British contemporary, Dr Nehemiah Grew, also recorded a description of fingerprints in *Philosophical Transactions*, 1684.

In 1823, Czech physiologist Jan Purkenje published a paper suggesting that fingerprints were unique to each individual human being. He described nine different patterns and suggested a method of classifying them, but it was too complicated to be of practical use for police forces.

In 1859, William Herschel, a young civil servant in India, was taking fingerprints instead of a signature to act as a system against fraud. He had realized that some retired Indian soldiers were in fact queuing up for their pensions more than once. To combat this fraud, their fingerprints were recorded in their pay book on each occasion they were paid. These records not only enabled checks to be made in relation to pensioners who were suspected of committing fraud, but also showed each of the retired soldiers' fingerprints in a series as they became older. William Herschel concluded, independently from Professor Purkinje, that human fingerprints were indeed unique to an individual and that they did not alter over a person's lifetime. He suggested that the Bengal

could rely upon the police officer having taken accurate measurements in the first place. At that stage, fingerprints acted as the final criterion of identification, once the other measurements had narrowed the field of suspects. In the early days, there was no reference system for a collection of complex fingerprint patterns: the fingerprint impressions were simply stored against each criminal's name.

FIRST USE OF FINGERPRINTS

Fingerprints could solve the question of a criminal's identification with his record, but could also help to trace an offender from marks left at the scene prison service adopt his system of classification and analysis, but they did not do so and Herschel returned to England in 1879.

In that same year, 1879, Dr Henry Faulds, a Scottish physiologist and medical missionary in Tokyo, had assisted in the case of a thief who had left his dirty handprint on a whitewashed garden wall. Faulds had been studying fingerprints, and proved that the man in police custody could not have been the culprit. The doubtless mixed feelings of the Japanese police became far more positive a few days later when another suspect confessed to the crime and was confirmed as the culprit because his handprint corresponded exactly with the mark left on the garden wall. Faulds wrote an article about fingerprints in the October 1880 issue of the journal *Nature,* in which he described the common patterns, and gave two examples of assisting criminal investigations.

It was Francis Galton, a gifted scientist and cousin of Charles Darwin, who used Herschel's Indian studies and his own research to calculate that the odds against any two individuals having identical fingerprints were 1 in 64,000 million. The uniqueness of fingerprints as an identifier thereby became established. By 1895, Galton had also devised a new system for classification, using the descriptions of 'arches' (5% of prints), 'loops' (60%) and 'whorls' or 'composites' (35%). There were still problems of simplifying the analysis for operational police use, however, particularly in relation to retrieving a matching set of prints from a large collection.

of a crime. The finding of a bloody fingerprint in 1892, at the scene of the murder of two young children in Argentina, became the first occasion when a murder case was solved with the assistance of fingerprints. Juan Vucetich, an officer in Buenos Aires, had read an article by Galton in *Revue Scientifique.* Vucetich had already reached his own conclusions about fingerprint patterns and had developed a ten-finger classification system of his own. Vucetich had pursued his theories without official finance, but all his efforts became immediately vindicated by this single case.

The mother of the two illegitimate children, 25-year-old Francesca Rojas, herself slightly wounded in the incident, had accused a neighbouring farmer named Velasquez of murdering the children, and the police began to investigate him because he was Francesca Rojas' man friend. There was no other evidence, and the police inquiries into such an emotional and traumatic case were at risk of going in completely the wrong direction. But Vucetich solved the case by demonstrating that the bloody fingermark found at the scene of the crime did not belong to Velasquez: it was in fact the fingerprint of Francesca Rojas herself. Francesca Rojas was confronted with this dramatic evidence and then confessed to killing her own children and to inflicting injuries on herself to divert suspicion. Her motive was connected with a condition of Velasquez's proposal of marriage to her: that she was not encumbered with the children. Vucetich achieved what Faulds had done in the Tokyo burglary case; he proved that one person was not the perpetrator of a crime, and also demonstrated that somebody else was the real culprit.

The cases investigated by Faulds and Vucetich involved people who were believed to have a connection with the crime, and where it was relatively easy to compare their fingerprints to confirm or disprove their involvement. The process of matching a fingermark with the thousands of others stored within a police file was a problem of a different scale, however.

It was this aspect of the problem that interested Edward Henry. In 1896, he was on home leave from his position as a senior officer in the Bengal police, and conferred with Galton about the subject of fingerprints. When Henry returned to India, he drew on the assistance of two of his most able officers, Hemchandra Bose and Azizul Hacque and they finally worked out a practical method of classification.

Henry wrote a book, *Classification and Uses of Fingerprints,* which was adopted by the Indian government as a text book. By the time of Henry's home leave in 1900, the Belper Committee, which was concerned about identification of criminals, had been established. Henry was able to demonstrate to this new committee how the effectiveness of his classification and retrieval system had overcome earlier difficulties. The committee recommended that anthropometry should be replaced by his system.

Henry's fingerprint classification system

Henry's method of classification (see plate 17) gave a numerical value to each of a person's fingers and thumbs, according to whether or not they featured a whorl pattern, and an overall two-figure classification was then calculated.

This was achieved by examining the prints from the digits of a person's hands, treating the ten prints as five pairs. A number was allocated to each digit with a whorl or composite pattern. Prints with a loop or arch were treated as zero. The numbers for whorls decreased from 16 for the first pair, 8 for the second, and so on down to 1 for the fifth pair.

Sir Harold Scott, in his book *Scotland Yard,* provides an example to illustrate the system, with the letter L signifying a digit with a loop pattern, whilst W indicates a whorl:

RIGHT HAND					LEFT HAND				
Thumb	Fore-finger	Middle	Ring	Little	Thumb	Fore-finger	Middle	Ring	Little
L	L	W	L	L	W	W	W	L	W
0	0	8	0	0	4	2	2	0	1
1st pair		2nd pair		3rd pair		4th pair		5th pair	

The score for each pair would then be arranged as if they were fractions, with the first of the pair above the line, and the second figure below it. The totals of all the numbers above the lines, and a separate total for all those below the lines would result in a two-figure classification. The example given above would end up like this:

0	8	0	2	0	and a total of	10
0	0	4	2	1		7

That overall two number classification would be one of a total of 1,024 possible permutations, a large enough number to act as a screening and reference system for a great number of fingerprints.

Once the fingerprints had been taken from an arrested suspect, they could be rapidly classified as one of the 1,024 categories, and the fingerprint officer could then turn to other fingerprints in that category, knowing that he would only have to compare a small number of prints in the relevant section to find out whether the suspect's prints were in the collection.

In due course, Henry sub-divided some of the larger groups within those categories, and other people later refined and developed the system.

THE FINGERPRINT BUREAU

Edward Henry had made a big impression. When a vacancy arose for Assistant Commissioner at Scotland Yard, he was duly appointed to the post, and lost no time in introducing the first Fingerprint Bureau in the United Kingdom on 1 July 1901.

Faulds and Vucetich had solved cases using fingerprints from crime scenes, but the primary purpose of the Bureau was to use fingerprints to ascertain whether those appearing before the courts had been in trouble before. This was the situation faced by Adolf Beck, who had been wrongly identified as the criminal John Smith. The effectiveness of the Fingerprint Bureau was demonstrated during the first six months of its life by making 93 identifications of criminals, far more than the anthropometric system that it was to replace.

However, the application of the fingerprint system to crime scene investigation was not forgotten. One of the three founding members of the Bureau, Detective Sergeant Charles Collins, studied photography in the belief that it should be possible routinely to record and examine fingermarks found at the scene of a crime. A photograph of fingerprints would identify the perpetrator if it were compared with fingerprints in the whole of the collection, not just against those of the suspect.

Collins' opportunity came in June 1902, when dirty fingermarks and a very clear impression of a left thumb were found on the newly painted window-sill of a burgled house in Denmark Hill, South London, where some billiard balls had been stolen. The police had no other evidence against any suspect. The marks were photographed and the Bureau's collection searched, using Henry's system. One can imagine the sense of triumph that arose when the thumb print was found to match that of a 41-year-old labourer and regular offender by the name of Harry Jackson (see plate 18). Henry's system had finally demonstrated its value in a real crime scene investigation. Jackson was then arrested, charged and sent for trial.

The prosecuting counsel at the Old Bailey, when Jackson appeared on 13 September 1902, was Richard Muir, who led an interested jury through a detailed explanation of the new system of fingerprints. Sergeant Collins gave evidence about his methods and the Fingerprint Bureau, and the jury then created history by making Jackson the first person in Britain to be convicted on fingerprint evidence. He was sentenced to seven years' penal servitude.

A month later in Paris, the murder of Joseph Reibel, a dentist's valet, provided the French police with a clue in the form of blood-stained fingerprints. The famous Alphonse Bertillon did not use Henry's classification system. He proceeded to work through many hundreds of fingerprints stored as an ancillary part of his bertillonage records. His triumph in identifying Henri-Leon Scheffer, recently arrived from Marseille, must have felt extremely gratifying – a vindication of his extreme patience, rather than Henry's retrieval system. Scheffer gave himself up to police before officers arrested him, and confessed to the murder.

The first British murder case solved by fingerprints happened nearly three years later, on 27 March 1905. Louis Kidman was a shop assistant in one of George Chapman's Oil and Colour shops, and shortly after 9am, went to the shop at Deptford to find out why it was still locked. Looking through the letter box of the shop door, he noticed that there was an overturned chair in the front parlour. With one of the other shop employees, he gained access to the back of the premises through the shop next door. To their horror, they found the shopkeeper, Thomas Farrow, lying dead in a pool of blood. When a police officer arrived, they ventured upstairs and found his wife, Ann, lying on a blood-stained bed, mortally wounded. Lying in the middle of the room was an empty cash box that would turn out to yield a vital clue. When it was examined, a clear blood-stained thumb mark was found.

Thomas Farrow had died about an hour earlier; at one stage he was seen standing by the shop door, suffering from head wounds. His wife, semi-conscious and deeply shocked from a fractured skull and a loss of blood, was taken to hospital where she died a few days later.

As the police made inquiries, they found that a milkman, Henry Jennings, had passed by at 7.15 that morning and had seen two men leave the shop and go off towards New Cross Road. He had whistled to them and told them that they had left the door open, but one of them had replied that it did not matter. Neither Mr Jennings, nor his 11-year-old assistant, could subsequently identify the men, but they did give their descriptions to the police. One wore a dark blue suit and a bowler hat; the other wore a dark brown suit, brown boots and a cap.

Another witness recognized a man she knew called Alfred Stratton, accompanied by another man, running across New Cross Road at about 7.15 that morning. She said that Alfred Stratton had been wearing a brown suit and the man with him had a bowler hat.

Alfred Stratton lived in Deptford in a room rented by Hannah Cromarty. Their landlady had treated Hannah Cromarty's black eye after she had been assaulted by Alfred on the Sunday evening immediately before the murder. The landlady had also seen Alfred's brother, Albert, wearing a bowler hat when he had been outside their house, before the two brothers had gone off together in the early hours of the morning. Later, she had seen Alfred fully dressed at 9.05am, while Hannah Cromarty was still in bed, and then saw Alfred putting black polish on his brown boots. After she heard about the murder, the landlady became suspicious about Alfred's involvement in the crime, not least because Hannah Cromarty had uncharacteristically done some washing.

A professional boxer who knew both Stratton brothers, had seen them together at about 2.30–3am near Deptford High Street, and a manure contractor's wife also knew Alfred Stratton and spoke to him in the area at 3.30am.

The police therefore had suspicions about the Stratton Brothers, but no evidence. At the Fingerprint Bureau, Detective Inspector Charles Collins examined the cash box and the thumb mark, but could not find any fingerprint in the collection at Scotland Yard that matched it.

Because of their movements near the scene of the crime, the police decided to arrest the Stratton brothers anyway. Sergeant Beavis found Alfred Stratton, on the Sunday following the murder, in the tap room of the King of Prussia public house in Deptford. Alfred asked whether he was wanted by police for living off the immoral earnings of Hannah Cromarty, but Sergeant Beavis told him that it was for another matter and asked him where his brother Albert was. Alfred replied that he had not seen Albert for a long time, and he might have gone to sea.

This was a classic case of the police searching for suspects whose fingerprints, once taken by police, would prove or disprove their contact with the murder scene. At Blackheath Road police station in Greenwich next morning, Charles Collins saw Alfred Stratton, and then set to work on a task that would create history, as his statement recounted:

> I have been attached to the Fingerprint Department since it was originated. We have in the Department now about 90,000 sets of finger prints. I have had ten years' experience in comparing finger prints for the purposes of identification. I have never in any case found as many as four points of identity to agree in the case of finger prints taken from two different individuals. The highest number I have found is three. When I have found four points of agreement and upwards they have always been the finger prints of the same individual.
>
> This cashbox was handed to me ... between five and six pm on the 27th March. On the side of the tray produced, I found a print of a digit, and I took a photograph of that, and I afterwards made an enlargement of that photograph.
>
> I endeavoured to find amongst the finger prints of the Department a print corresponding with that – but without success.
>
> On 3rd April I went to the Greenwich police station and took imprints of the digits of the prisoner Alfred Stratton, including the right thumb. I afterwards made a photographic enlargement of the imprint of his right thumb, and I compared that with the enlargement of the imprint on the cash box. Wherever it was clear I found it to agree. I have marked eleven points of agreement... There are other points of agreement which I have not numbered. I have no doubt whatsoever that the two imprints have been made from the same digit.   CRIM 1 98/5

The thumb mark on the cash box matched Alfred's right thumb, the first time in Britain that fingerprints had provided evidence in a murder case. Albert Stratton was arrested later, and the evidence that the two brothers had been together that night was sufficient to lead them to the dock at the Old Bailey on a charge of murdering Thomas and Ann Farrow (see plate 19).

The prosecuting barrister was, once again, Richard Muir, who had to explain the new science of fingerprints to another jury, one of whom had his fingerprints taken so that the rest of the jury could examine them. The evidence was contested by the defence medical experts, but the jury convicted both Stratton brothers of the crime and they were sentenced to death.

While the fingerprint evidence was being given, one of the interested observers in the courtroom was none other than Henry Faulds, who then wrote a letter to the Home Secretary explaining his long-term interest in the science of fingerprints. He admitted that he had offered his services to the defence with no fee in prospect, but had not been called as a witness. He picked holes in Charles Collins' evidence and made various suggestions about the criteria that should be applied to ensure that fingerprints could reliably be guaranteed to prove identity.

Although Fauld's suggestions were not taken up, the basis on which fingerprint experts would give evidence did in fact change over the following years. Early experts like Collins quoted how many fingerprints were in the collection, and how many comparisons they had made without finding a duplicated fingerprint. Collins found at least 11 points of agreement with Alfred Stratton's right thumb; in 1920, however, Scotland Yard introduced a standard of requiring a minimum of 16 characteristics of resemblance, and no features that were different. The number of characteristics could be reduced to 10, when more than one finger was involved. In 1953, these criteria eventually became a national standard. However, the effect of this standard meant that an incomplete but matching fingerprint found at the scene of a crime was sometimes too small to yield the requisite number of points of comparison and was therefore not produced as identification evidence for the court to consider. Within the last decade, the 16-point requirement has therefore been abandoned, and evidence of a fingerprint with fewer than 10 points of similarity can now be introduced into a prosecution case with a suitable explanation by an expert fingerprint officer.

Faulds himself became ever more deeply aggrieved by not being recognized for his part in the history of fingerprint science. Correspondence in the National Archives shows that the controversy lasted until well after his death, when a Mr George Wilton, a Lanarkshire lawyer, campaigned to persuade the Government to grant Faulds' daughters a pension. Sir Edward Henry wrote his own version of the history of the fingerprint system:

> Reviewing the work done by pioneers, I, in 'Classification and Uses of Fingerprints', published in 1900, came to the conclusion that PURKENJE, a Professor of Physiology who in 1820 [sic] read before the University of Breslau in Silesia a Latin treatise on Fingerprints, suggesting a system of classification and actually providing nine types for classification purposes, must be awarded the distinction of having originated the idea of Using Fingerprints in classified form.
>
> Sir William Herschel used the print of one finger to authenticate a document – he was an enthusiast – but did not attempt to tackle the subject of classification, but he collected a certain amount of material.
>
> Sir F. Galton took up Purkenje's idea and utilised Herschel's material in addition to what he himself had collected and devised a system of classification. He had 3 types instead of 9 like Purkenje and he relied for classification purposes on a system of suffixes. His system was ingenious but quite unsuited for a large collection. It took him, before Lord Belper's committee, nearly a dozen minutes to trace a duplicate in a collection of less than 2,500 – that is why it was made ancillary only to anthropometry in the system adopted up to 1901 in this country.
>
> In 1897, I had elaborated the system of classification in use in India and now in use everywhere and I had never even heard of Mr Faulds' name or labours in the field of research.   HO 144/788/128907

Despite his part in drawing attention to the potential of fingerprint science, Faulds' ideas were not accepted as any effective contribution to the development of a practical classification system for a large operational police collection. Herschel had apparently not thought of the use of fingerprints at crime scenes before Faulds had suggested it, and Galton seems either to have been unaware of, or to have failed to recognize Faulds' contribution. Already irritated by lack of recognition, Faulds would have been even more distressed if he had seen the official comment on the same file, 'This man is a crank'.

PALMPRINT IDENTIFICATION

By the time of the Stratton brothers' trial in 1905, Scotland Yard had registered 90,000 sets of fingerprints, and the number of identifications achieved by the Fingerprint Bureau had exceeded 5,000 cases by the end of 1904. Burglaries fell by 11% in 1904, perhaps as the result of criminals noting the fate of Harry Jackson.

The patterns of the ridges on our fingers are similar to those on our palms, and it was only a matter of time before a palmprint would secure a conviction equivalent to that of Harry Jackson or the Stratton brothers. The major problem was that only fingerprints were routinely taken from prisoners to prove their identity, and Scotland Yard did not have a large enough collection to make it likely that a suspect's palmprint would be stored in there.

The first time in which palmprint identification evidence was given in court was in 1931, when John Egan was prosecuted for a number of burglaries where fingerprints had led to his arrest. On a plate glass table at the scene of one of his burglaries, the burglar had left behind a clear palmprint, and when Egan's palmprints were taken when he was on remand in Brixton prison, Detective Inspector Frederick Cherrill compared them and proved that they were identical. Egan pleaded guilty, and the evidence was not contested, but the judge called Cherrill to the witness box to learn more about this development and to assure himself that palmprints were as infallible as fingerprints.

It was not until 30 April 1942 that the first disputed palmprint case arose. A 71-year-old pawnbroker by name of Leonard Moules had been found unconscious in Hackney Road, East London, with severe head injuries from which he later died. One of Scotland Yard's most experienced investigators, Detective Chief Inspector Ted Greeno, took charge of the case, and sought the assistance of Frederick Cherrill, by this time a Detective Superintendent (see plate 20). Inside Moules' safe, Cherrill found a palmprint that did not match the murdered man's or his assistant's. Nor did it match any of the 4,000 palmprints in Scotland Yard's collection.

The inquiry might have petered out, but one witness had seen two men near the scene whom he knew vaguely as 'George' and 'Sam'. In due course, the men were identified as George Silverosa and Sam Dashwood, who were then arrested as suspects. George Silverosa's palmprint matched the one found in the victim's safe, and the men's fate was sealed. Both blamed each other, and refused to give evidence at their trial, but they were convicted, and executed at Pentonville prison on 10 September 1942.

The identification of suspects, who could be arrested so that their fingerprints or palmprints could be examined, became a crucial element in cases like the Leonard Moules murder investigation. But where the police find an unidentified print at the scene of a major crime and there is no suspect, a serious problem arises. It is this type of situation that provides the argument for those who want the fingerprints of the whole population to be registered. Juan Vucetich in Argentina was one such advocate, and, with the experience of Vucetich's success in achieving the world's first murder conviction, Argentina did in fact introduce a law in 1916 to introduce compulsory fingerprint registration. The modern equivalent is the development of Britain's DNA database and the prospect of compulsory registration of biometric details for identity cards and passports. Argentina's law was subsequently abandoned in the face of a large section of the population, who not only refused to co-operate, but also protested violently against the measure.

One case where police had an unidentified palmprint was the murder of Mrs Elizabeth Currell, who was in the habit of walking her corgi dog on Potters Bar golf course. On 29 April 1955, she was attacked as she reached the 17th tee, and her body was found the next morning. The murder weapon had apparently been a heavy iron tee marker, on which police found part of a palmprint, of which there was again no trace in the Yard's collection. Other inquiries had led the police to believe that the offender worked or lived in the Potters Bar area, and the police took the decision to invite the male occupants of nearly 7,000 homes in the area to volunteer to give their palmprints for elimination purposes. By the middle of August, 9,000 palmprints had been taken. The group of specially assigned fingerprint officers were half way through the task of making comparisons, when a print was found to correspond to the mark on the murder weapon. That palmprint belonged to a youth named Michael Queripel, who lived with his parents close to the golf course. After his arrest, he admitted the murder and was detained 'during Her Majesty's pleasure', having become the first criminal detected as the result of a mass palmprinting exercise.

The enormous task of taking and comparing so many palmprints had been exceeded in scale by an inquiry that took place seven years earlier, when a horrific murder in Blackburn led to the first mass public fingerprint elimination exercise. In the early hours of 14 May 1948, a nurse in the children's ward at Blackburn's Queen's Park Hospital found that a child was missing: 4-year-old June Ann Devaney was found dead in the hospital grounds, having been sexually assaulted and battered to death.

The polished floor of the hospital ward revealed prints by stockinged feet, but the second clue came in the form of a bottle, which must have been moved by the murderer. The bottle was fortunately preserved for evidence and revealed fingerprints, but it then became necessary to eliminate anybody who might have been in that ward and touched the bottle for legitimate reasons. The fingerprints could not be matched from the police's fingerprint collection. With the assistance, again, of Frederick Cherrill of Scotland Yard, the police undertook the unprecedented step of fingerprinting the entire adult male population of Blackburn, and took more than 46,000 sets of fingerprints. Set number 46,253 belonged to Peter Griffiths, and matched those found on the bottle at the hospital. Griffiths was later convicted, and was hanged on 19 November 1948. If it had not been for the time-consuming and systematic process of taking and comparing so many fingerprints, it is probable that Griffiths would have remained free, perhaps to have killed another innocent child.

The establishment of the Fingerprint Bureau can justifiably claim to have been one of biggest factors in the enhancement of Scotland Yard's reputation in those critical first years of the 20th century, and the prospect of finding fingerprints transformed the methods used by the police for crime scene investigation.

CHAPTER EIGHT

Ship's radio catches a killer: the case of Dr Crippen

The infamous case of Dr Crippen has its own place in the annals of the country's crime stories, but few people could have predicted the turn of events that would give such a gruesome reputation to somebody who presented himself as such a mild-mannered medical man.

Hawley Harvey Crippen was an American, born in Coldwater, Michigan in 1862 and brought up in a strictly religious family. He qualified as a doctor in 1885, after gaining diplomas in Cleveland and New York, and then worked for a patent medicine company. His first wife, Charlotte, died in about 1890 and their son Otto was looked after by his grandparents.

Soon afterwards, Crippen met Cora Turner, an ambitious 19-year-old, who was being kept by a Mr Lincoln. When Cora told Crippen that her Mr Lincoln wanted her to go and live with him, Crippen proposed, and their marriage took place in Jersey City in September 1892. Cora's real name was Mackamotzki.

After a succession of jobs, Crippen moved to England in 1900 and Cora joined him later. In September 1905, the Crippens moved to 39 Hilldrop Crescent, Holloway, but their marriage was not happy. Cora was making determined efforts to break through to the fame that she thought she deserved in the music hall world. She acquired many friends through her outgoing personality and her involvement on the stage as 'Cora Motzki' and later 'Belle Elmore'. As her stage activity decreased, her involvement with the theatre turned to taking up the post of honorary treasurer of the Music Hall Ladies' Guild. She entertained gentleman friends at her home, where she slept in a different bedroom from her husband. Cora was better known by her stage name Belle Elmore, and Crippen, in turn, was often known as Peter.

A paying guest at the Crippen household, Karl Reinisch, described Cora's 'full, opulent figure', her ambition, and how she was a bad loser at cards. In 1906, when Herr Reinisch asked Cora whether he could extend his visit, he received a somewhat flowery note from her, excusing herself from being able to accommodate him, but inviting him to her 'weekly receptions' (see plate 21). This unremarkable correspondence later became not only an indication of Cora Crippen's projection of her own social standing, but also one of the sources by which Cora Crippen's authentic handwriting could be examined.

On one evening, 31 January 1910, the Crippens gave a small dinner party for two retired music hall artistes, Paul Martinetti and his wife Clara, followed by a game of whist. The Martinettis left at about 1.30am and were the last friends to see Cora Crippen alive.

CORA'S DISAPPEARANCE

Cora failed to attend her usual Wednesday meeting of the Music Hall Ladies' Guild on 2 February. The person who did attend was Ethel le Neve, Crippen's typist, with whom he had been having a secret affair. Ethel gave the committee two letters, signed in the name of Belle Elmore, but not in her handwriting. The letters recorded Mrs Crippen's sudden resignation, and informed them that she had had to go to America because of a relative's illness.

Cora's friends became anxious about her, but Dr Crippen told them that Belle was 'right up in the wilds of California', and, later, that she was suffering from double pneumonia. Crippen attended the Guild's Benevolent Fund dinner and ball, accompanied by Ethel le Neve who, through either naivety or brazenness, was wearing Belle's brooch and fur coat. Ethel's landlady had noticed how depressed Ethel had been in January, but how much more cheerful she had become in February. Ethel left her lodgings on 12 March, and gave Mrs

Jackson some clothing, telling her that *somebody* had gone away to America!

On 16 March, Crippen gave the landlord of Hilldrop Crescent three months' notice and, a week later, Crippen took Ethel on a holiday to Dieppe for a few days. On the day of their departure, Clara Martinetti received a telegram from Crippen, informing her of Cora's death, and a death notice duly appeared in *The Era,* a theatrical newspaper, on 26 March.

Two of Cora's friends, Mr and Mrs John Nash, had been touring American music halls, and made inquiries in the Los Angeles area, but without finding any record of Cora's death. After seeing Crippen on their return to England, they felt so uneasy that they went to Scotland Yard and told a senior detective, Chief Inspector Walter Dew, about their concerns.

Dew took up inquiries amongst the Crippens' former friends, and submitted a report on 6 July, stating, amongst other things, that the joint bank account operated by the Crippens had been paying out cheques up until 22 March, the day before Cora had, according to Crippen, been on her death bed in America.

Two days later, Walter Dew and Sergeant Mitchell called at Hilldrop Crescent, where a servant answered the door and brought them into the house. Ethel le Neve, again wearing Cora Crippen's brooch in the form of the rising sun, greeted them, saying that she was Dr Crippen's housekeeper. She became rather agitated on learning that Dew was from Scotland Yard, and then admitted that she was the doctor's typist. Dew insisted that he wanted to interview Dr Crippen as soon as possible, and eventually Ethel le Neve reluctantly agreed to accompany the officers to Crippen's business premises at Albion House, New Oxford Street.

At his office on the third floor of Albion House, Dr Crippen admitted to Dew that he had lied to his wife's friends, but his explanation may not have been what Cora's friends would have expected. Over the next five hours, Crippen made a long statement to the effect that Cora had left him for another man:

> After being questioned by Chief Inspector Dew as to the statements
> made by me that my wife, known as Belle Elmore, is dead, I desire to
> make a voluntary statement to clear the whole matter up...

When I returned [from America] I found she had been singing at Smoking Concerts for payment, and that an American Music Hall Artiste, named Bruce Miller, had been a frequent visitor to her at her house.

I may say that when she came to England from America her manner towards me was entirely changed, and she had cultivated a most ungovernable temper, and seemed to think I was not good enough for her, and boasted of the men of good position, travelling on the boat, who had made a fuss of her…

There were very frequent occasions when she got into most violent tempers and often threatened she would leave me, saying she had a man she could go to and she would end it all.

I have seen letters from Bruce Miller to her, which ended 'with love and kisses to Brown Eyes'…

On the Monday night the day before I wrote the letter to the Guild resigning her position as treasurer, Mr and Mrs Paul Martinetti came to our place to dinner, and during the evening Mr Martinetti wanted to go to the lavatory. As he had been to our house several times I did not take the trouble to go and show him where it was. After they had left, my wife blamed me for not taking him to the lavatory and abused me and said 'This is the finish of it. I won't stand it any longer. I shall leave you tomorrow and you will never hear of me again.'

She had said this so often that I did not take much notice of it, but she did say one thing which she had never said before; viz: that I was to arrange to cover up any scandal with our mutual friends and the Guild the best way I could. Before this she had told me that the man she would go to was better able to support her than I was.

I came to business the next morning, and when I went home between 5 & 6pm I found she had gone…

Whatever I have said to other people in regard to her death is absolutely wrong, and I am giving this explanation. So far as I know she is still alive.

We had a joint account at the Charing Cross bank, subject to the signature of either [sic] …and several blank cheques were always already signed by her.

She suffered from bilious attacks, and I have given her medicine for that – homeopathic remedies…

Miss Le Neve has been in my employ … I have been intimate with her during the past 3 years and have frequently stayed with her at Hotels, but was never away from home at night…

My belief is that my wife has gone to Chicago to join Bruce Miller.

MEPO 3/198

Ethel herself admitted living with Crippen as his wife since Cora had gone to America, and stated that she had been given some of Cora's furs to wear. Her moral position was delicate for a woman at that time, and, as she expanded her statement, her story must have seemed less and less likely. She had been 'astonished' to hear of Mrs Crippen's death, but 'did not think' that she had discussed it with Crippen. She 'could not remember' whether Crippen had originally told her that his wife was coming back from America or not, and 'could not remember' whether he had gone into mourning.

Crippen and Ethel then returned with Dew and Mitchell to Hilldrop Crescent, where the officers searched the house for clues to Cora's where-abouts, including giving a cursory look at the coal cellar. Dew noted that Cora had left much of her jewellery and clothes behind. He made it clear to Crippen that he would need to find Cora and helped Crippen to draft an advertisement for the American newspapers using Cora's maiden name of Mackamotzki. The advertisement requested Belle Elmore to 'communicate with HHC or Authorities at once. Serious trouble through your absence', and offered a $25 reward for information about her whereabouts. Crippen and Ethel le Neve appeared not to have grieved much for Cora, but was Crippen's wife really missing, as claimed by the doctor?

Dew spent the weekend circulating details of the missing woman and reviewing the evidence he had obtained. On the Monday, Dew again called at Albion House with the intention of seeing Crippen again, but found that he had disappeared, apparently with Ethel le Neve. The Chief Inspector now continued his inquiries with even greater vigour, and instigated a thorough search of the house, during which he found a loaded revolver. The house and garden were searched repeatedly and unsuccessfully over several days.

On the Wednesday, Dew challenged Crippen's business colleague, Mr Long, that he had not disclosed everything he knew, and Long then admitted that he had purchased a boy's suit for Crippen before his departure. This turned out to be the disguise used by Ethel.

Dew's report detailed the continuation of his search (see plate 22):

> On Wednesday 13th, I made enquiries in various directions and endeavoured to trace boxes said to have been removed from 39 Hilldrop Crescent, and again, with Sergeant Mitchell, went to that address and again dug several parts of the garden, and finally went to the coal cellar again, the flooring of which was brick.
>
> We went down on our hands and knees and carefully examined the brick flooring again, but everything appeared to be in order.
>
> We then got a small poker and tested various parts of the flooring of the basement, and probed about the brickwork of the cellar, and in doing so the poker, which has a thin point, went in between two of the bricks, which became loosened, and Sergeant Mitchell and I then removed several bricks and found, underneath, a flat surface of clay.
>
> I then procured a spade from the garden and dug, and on taking the surface up we found the earth somewhat loose, and after digging about three spadefuls I came across what appeared to be human flesh, but on account of the terrible smell, we had to cease our labours for a time.
>
> On resuming the digging we unearthed a large mass of flesh, and then sent for the Divisional Surgeon Dr Marshall and ACC. This would be about 5.30pm.   HO 144/788/128907

Walter Dew and Sergeant Mitchell had apparently solved the mystery of Cora's disappearance; they had found the remains of human flesh, but neither head nor bones were ever discovered. It is understandable that the discovery, six months after her death, caused the officers to resort to Dew's brandy to revive themselves before starting the next stage of their inquiries, which now formally became a murder case (see plate 23).

The remains were photographed by William McBride, an early police photographer, and were duly examined by the police surgeon and Professor Augustus Pepper. At a later stage, a 33-year-old pathologist, Bernard Spilsbury, became involved. It was Spilsbury's first big case, and he went on to become a famous expert witness whose every word seemed to be accepted by juries because of his status and reputation.

The conclusions were that the remains were of a stout female who had bleached her hair and who had undergone abdominal surgery in the past. As far as the cause of death was concerned, some of her organs contained enough hyoscine to have killed her. Hyoscine was a poison that could be taken in sweet tea or coffee. It could cause a person to become delirious, then drowsy, then unconscious, and to kill the victim within a dramatically changing process lasting about 12 hours. It was possibly the first time that this substance was used in a murder case, but much smaller doses had been in regular use, in asylums, to calm down violent patients.

Crippen had collected five grains of hyoscine from a chemist's, Lewis and Burrows of New Oxford Street, twelve days before the dinner party with the Martinettis. Crippen later testified that he had experimented with hyoscine in a nerve tonic in the proportion of 5/480th of a grain to a drop of water. His order from the chemist's would have been sufficient for over 500 doses at that rate; the amount in the dead body from Hilldrop Crescent would have been about half a grain, and certainly sufficient to have killed his wife.

The newspapers became transfixed with the case, and found more than enough excitement for a good story. The involvement of a music hall artiste, an American doctor, a dismembered body and an affair with a typist probably dressed as a boy, were a sensation.

ESCAPE BY SEA

The publicity certainly helped to trace the runaway couple who, immediately after leaving home, had made their way to the Continent. Twelve days after their interviews with Chief Inspector Dew, they set sail from Antwerp for Canada in the cargo ship *Montrose*. Crippen used the name John Philo Robinson, travelling with his 'son', John. The *Montrose's* captain was Henry George Kendall, who, when later claiming a reward, described in his statement how his suspicions were aroused. Crucially, his ship was equipped with a Marconi wireless transmitter that provided an opportunity to communicate the captain's suspicions to the ship's owners in Liverpool (see plate 24):

I sailed from Millwall docks, London, on the *Montrose* at 6pm July 14th 1910.

On July 13th the Thames Police supplied me with a full written description of Crippen, wanted in London for murder, in which it was stated that Le Neve might be dressed as a boy in a brown suit of clothes...

I saw the passengers come on board at Antwerp, but my particular attention was not attracted to any of them. Whilst waiting for my ship to sail from Antwerp, I purchased a Continental edition of the *Daily Mail*, and there saw the photos and description of Le Neve and Crippen.

Three hours after sailing, and when 30 miles from Flushing, my attention was attracted to the two persons whom I now know to be Crippen and Le Neve, by the supposed boy squeezing the elder man's hand near one of the boats... When I saw the boy squeeze the man's hand I thought it strange and unnatural, and it occurred at once to me that they might be Crippen and Le Neve.

I wished them the time of day and took a keen observation of all points, and felt quite confident that they were the persons wanted.

I did not do anything further that day or take any steps because I wanted, before raising an alarm, to make sure I was making no mistake...

On the 22nd Friday, I entered into conversation with Crippen (who was travelling in the name of Mr Robinson, and Le Neve as Master Robinson) regarding sea sickness amongst passengers, and the remedies they carried for curing same. In answer to my observations he used some medical terms for certain remedies.

I was then fully convinced that he was a medical man.

I also noticed that Mr Robinson was flat on the bridge of his nose as described in Police circulation, and that there was a deep mark on the nose as if caused by spectacles.

I also noticed that Crippen spoke quietly in French to two French passengers opposite him, and Police description mentioned that Crippen spoke French.

I was then positively convinced that it was Crippen and Le Neve and I sent for Mr L. Jones my Marconi operator, and told him to send the following message at once:

Piers. Liverpool

3pm Greenwich mean time

Montrose. 130 miles West of Lizard

Have strong suspicion that Crippen London Cellar Murderer and accomplice are amongst saloon passengers. Moustache shaved off, growing beard. Accomplice dressed as boy. Voice, manner and build undoubtedly a girl.

Kendall

I continued to keep them under observation and they were at my table, and the more I saw of them the more I was convinced, and I sent a further Marconi as to the identity, *'passengers not suspicious, am keeping everything quiet. Have sent full report by SS Montezuma from London to owners at Liverpool.*

The next thing, I got a wireless message from Chief Inspector Dew, on board *Laurentic*, and he and I constantly communicated with each other (from Father Point) and made mutual arrangements as to his boarding the Montrose. HO 144/788/128907

Most of the 280 passengers on the *Montrose* travelled 'steerage' in converted cargo holds; only 20, like Mr Robinson and his 'son', had second-class tickets. There were no first-class passengers, and so it was not unlikely that the couple would attract attention. In addition to his other observations, Captain Kendall noticed that the voice of Mr Robinson's 'son' began in a low register and became progressively higher. His clothes appeared to be ill-fitting, especially where a young man would not be expected to display curved flesh.

When the ship's owners received Captain Kendall's message, they notified the Liverpool police. On the evening of Friday 22 July, Walter Dew excitedly went by cab to the home of his Assistant Commissioner, Sir Melville Macnaghten. The two men discussed what action they should take about this unknown sea captain's suspicions. Might it be simply another case of mistaken identity?

Dew wanted to chase Crippen to Canada. The White Star liner *Laurentic* was due to sail from Liverpool the following day, with a seven-day scheduled voyage time. The *Montrose's* voyage would take 11 days, but three days had effectively already passed, and there could be no further delay if Dew were to catch them. Decisiveness won the day. Sir Melville gave his authority, and Dew's dramatic pursuit began. Using the alias Mr Dewhurst in an attempt to keep his presence confidential (see plate 25), Dew was virtually the last passenger to board the *Laurentic,* and a week of suspense about the outcome then began. The newspapers maintained an excited commentary on the progress of the two ships, whilst Scotland Yard made further inquiries to try to confirm or disprove Captain Kendall's suspicions.

The chase across the Atlantic had echoes of the actions of Richard Tanner's pursuit of Franz Müller 46 years earlier, but it would not have been possible without the new invention of the Marconi wireless telegraph. In addition to all the other advantages of the new equipment, it had established for the first time that the invention could be used from a ship to catch a fugitive criminal at sea.

The better speed of the *Laurentic* had its desired effect, and on the morning of Sunday 31 July, Dew boarded the *Montrose* wearing the jacket and cap of the pilot service, accompanied by Canadian police officers. He greeted Dr Crippen on the deck with a 'Good morning!' and any remaining doubts about the identity of the passenger disappeared. Ethel le Neve was in her cabin.

After three weeks in Montreal, the party travelled back to England on the *Megantic* (see plate 26). When Dew and his prisoners arrived back in England, they were greeted by large crowds who booed Crippen. The trial opened at the Old Bailey on 18 October 1910 before Lord Alverstone, the Lord Chief Justice. Richard Muir, who had gained fame through the first fingerprint trials, was the prosecuting barrister and his opposite number, Aspinall Tobin, appeared for the defence, managed by solicitor Arthur Newton. Newton was subsequently suspended from practice for selling a forged letter from Crippen to the magazine *John Bull.*

Crippen denied murdering his wife, and relied on his first statement to Walter Dew that Cora had gone to America and might be still alive. But the jury accepted the evidence that the remains under the coal cellar floor belonged to Cora, and, in particular, Spilsbury's explanation that the mark on the flesh was consistent with a surgical operation known to have been carried out in America to remove her ovaries: the defence claimed that the mark was simply a fold in the skin. In February that year, shortly after Cora's demise, Crippen had bought some lime, presumably to help her remains to decompose more quickly. His story about only using hyoscine for legitimate purposes was not given much credence. Cora's remains were also accompanied by part of Crippen's pyjamas.

After a five-day trial, the jury retired for only 27 minutes before convicting Crippen who, despite protesting his innocence, was given the death sentence. This was carried out on 23 November 1910.

In the meantime, Ethel was tried separately, and wisely instructed different defence solicitors. Her trial lasted only one day. She did not give evidence and, doubtless assisted by Crippen's statements of her innocence, she was acquitted.

Whatever Crippen's plans for a life in Canada might have been, a card found in his possession indicated the depths of despair he had been feeling at one stage. The card, which Ethel apparently never received, said, 'I see nothing bright ahead and money has come to an end. I have made up my mind to jump overboard tonight. I know I have spoil[ed] your life but I do hope some day you can learn to forgive me. With last words of love, your H' (*The People's Journal and Angus Herald,* 23 February 1935). Nonetheless, if it had not been for the Marconi equipment on board the *Montrose,* Crippen would have had the opportunity to start a new life in Canada.

JOHN TAWELL

Wireless communications became an indispensable part of police work, but, using cable connections, the telegraph had in fact already been used 65 years beforehand on land to catch a murderer, in the case of a man in Quaker dress known as John Tawell. Tawell travelled to London on the evening of 1 January 1845 from Slough, after he had murdered his mistress, Sarah Hart. He was travelling on the 7.42pm from Slough, and had been seen on the train. The Great Western Railway police telegraphed Tawell's description ahead to Paddington station, from where Sergeant William Williams of the railway police followed Tawell to an address in the City of London, where Tawell lodged for the night. Setting an example for the hapless Sergeant

McBride in the Mapleton case 36 years later, Sergeant Williams reported his actions, but did not detain Tawell or keep a watch on the premises. By the time Inspector Wiggins of the Metropolitan Police's D Division went to arrest Tawell the next morning, the suspect had left. Assisted no doubt by Tawell's distinctive garb, however, Wiggins soon traced him to the Jerusalem Coffee House and arrested him for murder.

Tawell's appearance may have been that of a religious man of saintly character, but his antecedents told a different story. On 16 February 1814 he had been sentenced to transportation to Australia for 14 years, departing on the *Marquess of Wellington* convict ship, after attempting to deceive an engraver into making up a plate to print bank notes for the Uxbridge Bank. Tawell had, like Crippen, used poison, but he had chosen prussic acid. In those days, substances now regarded as murderous poisons could be obtained relatively easily in chemists' shops. Prussic acid can also be produced by cyanide, a natural vegetable acid which can result in some of the fastest deaths by poison. An expert chemist found no fewer than 50 grains of prussic acid in Sarah Hart's stomach, an amount which could easily have caused her death.

Wireless telegraph equipment was an excellent advance in communications on land as well as on the sea. The police officers circulating their route papers about Daniel Good may have envied the speed of the telegraph used to catch Tawell only three years later in 1845; but they would surely have been thoroughly amazed at the wireless technology that enabled a ship at sea to help Walter Dew's pursuit of Crippen.

CHAPTER NINE

Ballistics breakthrough:
the gun's signature revealed

As science and technology progressed, so the study of ballistics developed, until it became possible to link a bullet to a certain make of firearm, and then to an individual gun. The methodical study of evidence relating to firearms was taking place well before the advent of Scotland Yard, however. As far back as 1794, a surgeon removed and preserved a wad of paper from the gunshot wound suffered by a Lancashire man, Edward Culshaw. When the paper was unfolded, it was found to match the missing torn-off corner of a ballad sheet still in the pocket of the suspect, John Toms.

Sixty-six years later, on 24 October 1860, PC Alexander McBrian, a police officer in Wyberton, Lincolnshire, was shot by Thomas Richardson, a suspected poacher, and the case was solved by similar means, as reported in *The Times*:

> Thomas Richardson, labourer, charged with the wilful murder of Alexander McBrian, by shooting at him on the 25th October, at Wyberton, and also charged with the same offence upon the coroner's inquisition, pleaded 'Not guilty'...
>
> The deceased, a policeman, was on duty on the night of the 24th October... Noticing that there was something bulky in the pocket of the man's jacket, McBrian called to him, 'Holloa! What are you off with

there?' The man upon this turned round, and, as McBrian said, 'shot slap into me...'

On the following morning, about 8, Superintendent Manton and another police constable went to the house of the prisoner, which was about 450 yards distant from the spot where the shot had been fired, and there found a double-barrelled gun, the left barrel of which was still loaded, while the right had all the appearance of having been discharged within 24 hours... An endeavour was made to draw out the charge from the left barrel of the gun, but, this failing, it was discharged into the ground, and the paper which had been used as wadding was picked up, and, on being examined, appeared to be portions of a newspaper...

Some pieces of printed paper, charred at the edges and having a smell of gunpowder, or sulphur, were found by Superintendent Manton on the spot where McBrian had been wounded, and the collation of these with those discharged from the left barrel of Richardson's gun formed the damning evidence in the case. Mr Thomas Cope, the publisher of *The Times,* who was also its publisher in 1854, proved that the pieces of paper found in the churchyard, and also those that had come from the left barrel of the gun, had formed part of *The Times* newspaper of the 27th March of that year...

Four days after McBrian was wounded, the prisoner was brought before him and recognized as the man who had discharged the gun. McBrian had been hopeful of recovery, but growing worse and his case hopeless, he was told by his medical attendant that his chances of recovery were very poor. He replied that it was a very bad case; a bad job... If I am a dying man, the prisoner is the man who shot me.

The Times, 10 December 1860

Twelve years before the Harriet Buswell murder case, there was no mention of an identification parade, perhaps because PC McBrian was too ill, but Richardson was convicted and sentenced to death. He subsequently confessed to the crime and was reprieved.

EARLY BALLISTIC EVIDENCE

Early firearms were invariably loaded from the muzzle, and ammunition was sometimes homemade. The Bow Street officer, Henry Goddard, described one of his cases in Southampton that occurred in 1835, nearly six years after the formation of the Metropolitan Police, but before the Southampton force had been established. Mrs Maxwell of Southampton had been the victim of a burglary, during which a firearm had been discharged. Her butler, Joseph Randall, had reported that he had challenged the burglars and, in an exchange of gunfire with the thieves, the gallant butler had apparently prevented the booty from being removed from the premises.

Goddard was suspicious of Randall's story, and asked to see his guns, ammunition and equipment. He was also given the bullet that had supposedly been fired at the butler. When Goddard examined these back in his hotel room, he found an identical pimple on all the bullets, including the one that had allegedly been fired at Randall. He then found a corresponding pinhead-sized hole in the mould from which Randall had made the bullets. This indicated that the bullet fired at Randall was in fact part of his own ammunition.

Goddard had his suspicions confirmed by the local gun-maker, and Randall was duly arrested. In prison, Randall confessed to making up the story with a view to obtaining a reward from his mistress for his bravery in protecting her property, and was eventually released with a sharp warning from the court. Goddard's keen observation had linked a series of bullets together.

The Metropolitan Police also came to use bullets as evidence. On 1 December 1882, when PC George Cole caught a young thief trying to break into a chapel in Dalston, his prisoner escaped by firing a pistol at him and PC Cole was killed. The offender left behind a chisel with the letters 'rock' scratched on it, and a hat, but despite these pieces of evidence, initial inquiries ground to a halt.

More than a year later, however, there was a breakthrough. Inspector Thomas Glass of N Division, received some information from Mr Billingshurst, whose wife was friends with Mrs Orrock and had come to believe that Thomas Orrock might have committed the murder. Inspector Glass suddenly realized that the letters scratched on the chisel could be part of Thomas Orrock's name. An enlarged photograph of the chisel revealed all the letters of Orrock's name, and the police then had a definite suspect in sight. They still needed firm evidence however, and knowing that Mrs Orrock would not willingly give information directly, Inspector Glass concocted a fictitious anonymous letter that he showed to Mrs Orrock, who then said she thought that a man named Ames had written it! Inspector Glass traced Ames, who led him to the accomplices who had been out with Orrock that night.

Orrock himself was then in gaol for another matter and Sergeant Cobb, who as a constable had been on duty with George Cole on the night he was shot, identified Orrock from amongst a group of other prisoners in Cold Bath Fields prison. Cobb also followed up information from Frederick Miles, who had seen Orrock practising with his new gun on Tottenham Marshes.

Sergeant Cobb found a mark in the tree pointed out by Miles, and managed to dig out a bullet that proved to be of the same type and weight as those recovered from PC Cole's body. James Squires, a gun-maker of Whitechapel, testified that the bullet from Tottenham Marshes and the two bullets from the scene were all of a type fired from the pin fire cartridges used by the gun that had been bought (and later thrown away) by Orrock. The trial, which ended in Orrock's conviction and execution for murder at Newgate on 6 October 1884, was probably the earliest recorded use of ballistics evidence by the Metropolitan Police.

THE MOAT FARM MURDER

In March 1903, Scotland Yard was asked to help the local police with inquiries into the disappearance of the wealthy Miss Camille Cecile Holland from her home at Moat House Farm, Clavering in Essex. She had been living with Samuel Dougal, and had paid for the farm herself in April 1899. Dougal had been married three times before, had a conviction for forgery and, at one stage, had been admitted to a mental asylum. Nobody saw Camille Holland after June 1899, but seven cheques had been drawn from her London bank account since her disappearance, on every occasion corresponding to amounts paid into Dougal's account. As inquiries gathered pace, Dougal apparently felt that the net was starting to close in on him, and disappeared from the farm.

A warrant was issued for Dougal's arrest for the forgery of Camille Holland's signature, and he was caught on 18 March 1903 and remanded in custody. The police then began to search for Camille Holland's body at the farm. On 27 April, officers succeeded in finding her body buried in a former drainage ditch.

Mr Pepper, an eminent pathologist from St Mary's Hospital London, conducted the post-mortem examination and found a revolver bullet that had entered her skull behind her right ear, fracturing the inside of her skull on the left side but without passing through the bone. Mr Edwin Churchill, who owned a gun shop in London, was called in to help. He had experience of giving expert evidence on behalf of the prosecution, and confirmed that the bullet recovered from Miss Holland's head was the same type as a box of 34 unused .32 calibre bullets also found at the farm.

Churchill said that the revolver must have been fired at a distance of between 6 and 12 inches from the victim's head. He came to this conclusion by systematically firing bullets into sheep's heads, with the assistance of his nephew Robert, to calculate the pattern of bullet penetration. The question of powder burns, the classic evidence of a shot from close range, could not be assessed because the flesh had disappeared in the four years since Miss Holland's death. In due course, the ballistics evidence helped to convict Samuel Dougal of the murder, the culmination of an excellent investigation by Detective Inspector Eli Bower of Scotland Yard. Dougal's solicitor, Arthur Newton, had to defend himself against an accusation that he had wrongly received payment from a newspaper in relation to this case, a complaint similar to one when he later defended Dr Crippen, a case in which the same pathologist, Mr Pepper, would also be involved.

THE 'HOODED MAN' CASE

It was on 9 October 1912, however, that a landmark case involving firearms occurred in Eastbourne, Sussex, at the house of Countess Flora Sztaray, where Police Inspector Arthur Walls was shot dead. The servants raised the alarm, but the culprit escaped, leaving behind his unusual size 7¼ trilby hat. The Eastbourne police alerted London to watch for suspects arriving by train, especially at Victoria, and Detective Chief Inspector Eli Bower, who had investigated the Moat Farm murder nine years earlier, took up the case:

When the Countess entered the house, she telephoned to the East-bourne Police, informing PC John Luck that there was a man lying on the porch over the front door, and asking for assistance to be sent... Before his arrival PC Luck received another message from the Countess enquiring if a man had been sent, and was informed, 'The Parade Inspector has been sent and should be there about now...'

The Inspector [arrived] ... and then apparently saw the man, as he requested him to come down.

Instead of doing so the man sat up and deliberately shot the Inspector in the left breast through the heart, with the result that he staggered out into the roadway, fell and died there, without, so far as can be ascertained, having spoken...

Dr G. Flanigan, who resides nearby, was called to attend the Inspector, but he could do nothing for him as death took place in a very short time...

The same evening, a man who gave the name of Doctor Power ... informed me that he knew the murderer to be one Frank Seymour... He said that Seymour, now known as John Williams, had recently resided in the vicinity of Finsbury Park. MEPO 3/226

The informant 'Doctor Power' stated that he knew the murder had been committed by John Williams, who carried a revolver. He said that Williams had recently been injured in a burglary in Bournemouth. Power was giving the police important information about the case, but they wondered what his motives were. Eli Bower suspected that Power had designs on Florence Seymour, the attractive (and pregnant) 'wife' of the suspect Williams. So the police used Power's information, but also kept him under secret surveillance as a check on his reliability.

The following day, whilst Florence Seymour and Power were deliberatly left alone together in an office at Scotland Yard, Florence destroyed a significant clue by throwing a cloak room ticket into the fire. Power was quick enough to read the number, however, and later told the police. This ticket number led them to Victoria Station's left luggage office where they found a portmanteau and a belt with a revolver holster – but no gun.

Power's role as an informant was bearing fruit: his information had led to the recovery of the holster. He also led police to Williams himself by alerting them to an arrangement he had made to meet Williams in the buffet of Moorgate station. Whilst the two men were engaged in conversation, Eli Bower and two other officers pounced on Williams and arrested him. Williams was told that he was being arrested for the Eastbourne murder, but protested his innocence. The prime suspect was therefore in custody, but there was no evidence or any admission by him to support a prosecution.

Eli Bower's next step was to try to gain more evidence from Florence Seymour. The officer intercepted her in Victoria Street as she was about to enter a restaurant, and took her to his office again. She was reluctant to give any statement, but, partly as the result of Power's persuasion, she did admit that on the evening of the murder she had gone with her husband to the top of South Cliff Avenue, Eastbourne. Williams had then left her for 20 to 30 minutes, wearing a soft, felt trilby hat, but did not have his hat when he returned. The label of the hat recovered at the scene of the crime showed that it had been purchased in Bournemouth, the town where, according to Power, Williams had recently been indulging in burglary.

Eli Bower was beginning to build his case, and Florence's account, if she held to it, would place Williams in the vicinity of the murder, but there was very little evidence against him. He had not been identified by witnesses, there were no fingerprints, and the murder weapon had not been recovered. Eli Bower's report shows that it was again through Power that the murder inquiry was rescued from potential failure:

> We have never lost touch with Power, and through him we were informed that the pistol had been buried somewhere on the beach at Eastbourne, but it was impossible for us to find it without some clear indication of its whereabouts. Power, however, succeeded in inducing the prisoner's wife to come to Eastbourne on the 15th instant, and he accompanied her... She was kept under observation... She remained on a certain seat for some considerable time but there were a good many people passing to and fro and it was evident that she was uneasy.
>
> She left the front, entered a cab and drove to the General Post

Office , where Power met her... It was then arranged that he [Power] should go with her to the beach and endeavour to find the revolver. This they did, but they were unsuccessful in their search. I therefore informed her that she would have to go to Eastbourne Police Station...

I said 'Where have you been in Eastbourne?' She replied 'On the front.' I said 'What were you doing there?' and before I could obtain any reply, she fainted... At her request Power was permitted to see her alone. Shortly afterwards she informed me that she desired to make a statement and tell me the whole truth ...

She admitted that she is not married to the prisoner...

In consequence of the statement made by her, Inspector Parker, Sergeant Hayman and I obtained lamps and proceeded to the spot where she herself had been searching, and after considerable labour we, in the early hours of the morning, succeeded in recovering the revolver in two parts, minus the hammer and two screws, which corroborates the woman's statement.   MEPO 3/226

The police had found parts of a gun without its hammer. But could Eli Bower prove that this was the weapon that had killed Arthur Walls?

Edwin Churchill had died in 1910, and his nephew Robert Churchill (see plate 27) had taken over the gunshop business, so Eli Bower asked for his expert opinion. Robert Churchill concluded, from the bullet that killed Arthur Walls and a cartridge case recovered from the scene, that the weapon had been a .25 automatic pistol. The police gave Churchill the gun components that they had found on the beach and Churchill assembled them, and, with the assistance of a new hammer and springs, test-fired the gun.

By examining bullets fired from the gun found on the beach, Churchill was able to draw conclusions about the gun's rifling marks. The rifling in a gun barrel is a system of grooves that make the bullet spin, and therefore travel straighter. The test bullets had the same rifling pattern as the bullet used to kill Inspector Walls, and Churchill had no doubt about his conclusions that it was a gun of that very same make that had fired the fatal bullet.

In order to demonstrate the technicalities of Churchill's evidence, Sergeant

William McBride, one of the very first police photographers at Scotland Yard, used close-range photography to illustrate the pattern of the grooves on the bullets. They also took an impression, using dentist's wax, of the inside of the gun barrel. McBride photographed the pattern in the wax caused by the grooves of the *inside* of the gun barrel, which showed the profile matching a lead bullet fired through that gun barrel. McBride spent a long time rotating the bullet until he could finally fit the two patterns together and demonstrate how the rifling patterns matched exactly. Churchill and McBride used the same method to create nine casts from other gun barrels to show the variations between different makes of firearms, and were thus able to explain a very technical matter to the jury in a simple and graphic way (see plate 28).

Williams and Florence Seymour were found to have in their possession a number of items of property stolen from houses in the region. Williams was convicted of the murder in a classic case that demonstrated the use of a wide variety of skills and methods to bring a difficult case to a successful prosecution. When Williams was being escorted into court, Eli Bower placed a spotted apron over Williams' head, since at that stage he had not been formally identified, and the trial then became known in the newspapers as the 'hooded man case'. John Williams was not his real name. He had enlisted into the Royal Scots Regiment (No 6910) as George McKay on 9 October 1899 and had deserted on 15 October 1901.

After the trial, Edgar Power, who had given such crucial information and direct assistance leading to Williams' conviction, successfully claimed the reward money, but, worried that he would spend it all too quickly, he asked for payment to be delayed until immediately before he left the country for America. Eli Bower had achieved a successful conclusion to a case that at one stage looked hopelessly weak. It was a milestone in the presentation of ballistic evidence to prove the make of gun involved in a crime from its rifling marks.

THE COMPARISON MICROSCOPE

In due course, the comparison microscope enabled ballistics experts to rotate two bullets and compare their rifling patterns with each other much more effectively. Sydney Smith, while working in Egypt, improvised a comparison microscope when, in November 1924, he was investigating the murder

Rifling marks

In 1889, Alexandre Lacassagne, at the University of Lyons, suggested that the scratches to be found on bullets recovered from the victims of gunshot wounds could potentially be matched with the original firearm, provided that the gun itself could also be recovered. He was investigating a case in which a gun, recovered in a suspect's home, had the seven rifling grooves within the barrel that matched the number of grooves of the bullet. These grooves are machined into the inside of gun barrels in a twisting pattern to make the bullets spin, and therefore travel straighter. The spaces between the grooves are known as *lands*.

In due course, it became possible for an expert to examine a spent bullet, to reach a conclusion about which types of gun could have fired the bullet from its size, and then to narrow down the possible makes of gun by identifying the number, size and direction of the grooves of the rifling of the gun barrel. Even apparently smooth metal inside a gun barrel has tiny machine marks that will leave a corresponding pattern on the bullet that can be seen under a microscope. Eventually, the smaller machine marks were shown to be unique to each individual gun barrel, a significant advance over the pattern of the rifling grooves simply indicating the make of gun.

Occasionally, distinctive faults, unique to a particular gun, would create their own identifying signature on bullets, in much the same way as the ammunition mould used by Randall the butler had created the unusual pimple noted by Henry Goddard.

A ballistics expert therefore needed the magnifying lenses and skill to make detailed observations, but also the comprehensive knowledge of the specifications of all firearms in production. In America, Charles Waite established an international reference collection of firearms and specifications, and, with Philip Gravelle, founded the world's first Bureau of Forensic Ballistics in New York in 1923. Two German experts, Hees and Haslacher, compiled an *Atlas of Arms*, which was an index of details of the world's firearms, whilst in England, Robert Churchill accumulated an encyclopaedic knowledge of firearms by examining and using the vast number of guns that he saw through his uncle's business. Churchill also catalogued the grooves, lands, pitch and twist of the rifling of every known make of revolver and automatic pistol. There was nobody in the British police service at the time who possessed any comparable technical knowledge.

in Cairo of Sir Lee Stack Pasha, the Commander-in-Chief and Sirdar of the Egyptian army.

Sydney Smith's microscopic examination and comparison of bullets was able to show that one .32 calibre weapon was involved in the Sirdar's assassination and, indeed, a whole series of political murders since 1919. The mark on the bullets was so distinctive that Smith became sure that he would be able positively to identify the weapon if it ever came into his laboratory. Eventually the gang were arrested with their firearms, one of which had a rust mark in the barrel that created exactly the same distinctive mark on bullets, thus proving the involvement of that weapon. Faced with this evidence, the gang confessed.

At about this time, Hugh Pollard, an associate of Robert Churchill, was experimenting with two microscopes linked together. Churchill himself went to America in 1927 to study American ballistics methods, and on his return, he commissioned Messrs Watsons of High Holborn to make a Comparison Microscope Mark II to a specification that he had drawn up with Pollard. The instrument was therefore available for a notorious murder that occurred later that year.

BROWNE AND KENNEDY

On 27 September 1927, a post office worker, Bill Ward, was driving in Essex, near Howe Green, early in the morning, when he saw the dead body of a police officer lying in the lonely country lane. The officer was PC George Gutteridge, whose pocket book and helmet were on the ground near his body. His pencil was clenched in his right hand. He had been shot four times in the face, including through both eyes. Nearby, a grass bank had been marked by something like a motor car wheel being driven firmly against it. There was no house within quarter of a mile of the scene, and nobody had heard anything to help the investigation. It appeared as if the officer had been shot while investigating a suspect travelling along that lonely road. Within a few hours, Scotland Yard had been called in.

Detective Chief Inspector James Berrett set off with Sergeant Harris in one of Scotland Yard's new Lea Francis cars to Romford, Essex, where he established his base to investigate the murder. The only other incident that had occurred that night was the theft of a Morris Cowley motor car from the garage of a Dr Lovell in Billericay, 10 miles away. Later that evening, the car was found in Brixton, London, and the inquiry then moved to trying to trace London criminals who might have committed such a crime.

The nearside mudguard of Dr Lovell's car had been damaged and there appeared to be some tree bark stuck to the front of the springs that protruded ahead of the radiator, which suggested that the car might have run into a bank by the roadside. There were blood splashes on one of the running boards. The car's mileometer showed that it had been driven 42 miles – about the distance from Dr Lovell's garage to Brixton. The car may have been driven along small roads to reduce the risk of detection on major routes into London.

But much more significant was a cartridge case marked RLIV under one of the seats. This marking indicated that it was an old Mark IV type bullet made at the Royal Laboratory in Woolwich Arsenal for troops in the First World War.

This ammunition had been discontinued after arguments that it contravened the Hague Convention on soft ammunition. When the cartridge case was properly examined in detail, it was found to have been scarred with a tiny, unusual mark, probably caused by a cleaning rod damaging the breech shield of the weapon that had fired it.

The bullets recovered from George Gutteridge's body and the scene of the crime were too deformed to allow comparison of the most detailed rifling marks, but they were sufficiently preserved for Robert Churchill to determine that it was a Webley revolver that had fired them.

The murder hunt went on for over three months without an arrest. Two Webley revolvers were found in the River Thames, but Churchill proved that neither could have been the murder weapon because they did not make the same distinctive mark on their cartridge cases.

In January of the next year, however, DCI Berrett was able to report on some significant developments. The *News of the World* of 15 January 1928 had published an appeal from PC Gutteridge's mother for people to come forward with information, and the newspaper had doubled its reward to £2,000. The Sheffield City police had reported that one of Berrett's suspects, Frederick Guy Browne, had resumed his old habits of stealing motor cars, including one from a Mrs Bridget Hutton of Tooting.

Mrs Hutton travelled to Sheffield and positively identified her car, which had been taken from her garage two months earlier. Despite being high up on the list of suspects, Browne himself had been elusive. As well as stealing cars, he had also committed a robbery at Eynsham railway station where an Olivetti typewriter was stolen.

Armed with this information, the police decided to move in, and lay in wait at Browne's garage at Clapham Junction. They knew that Browne himself had gone to Dartmoor prison to collect a young prisoner who was being released after serving his sentence. Browne returned to his garage on the evening of 20 January 1928, and was arrested:

> Upon arrest Browne was found to be in possession of a stockingette mask to cover the head completely, and also 12 rounds of .455 revolver ammunition, a pair of artery forceps and a wonderful skeleton key amongst other property on his person.
>
> In the car, in which he drove up to the garage, PC Beavis, CID W, found a Webley Mark VI revolver no 351931 fully loaded, in the offside pocket by the driver's seat, more skeleton keys, another pair of artery forceps, a torch and a jemmy. These articles were shown to DD Insp Leach by Det. Beavis in presence of Browne and the latter remarked, 'Ah. You've found that have you. I'm done for now.'
>
> When he was arrested Browne asked to go to the lavatory and simulated the appearance of abdominal pains, but was not allowed to go until some time later, when he was carefully escorted there. I would point out that the lavatory is in the garage yard and quite close to the car which Browne returned to the garage in, and it is highly probable that his intention was to get to the car and obtain possession of another fully loaded Webley revolver no 299431 which was found in this car in a cupboard at the rear of the driver's seat...
>
> At 33a Sisters Avenue in a room occupied by Browne, Sergeant Miller, W Division, found a small plated .22 six chambered revolver no 16769, fully loaded, in a leather bag... Detective Haines found another revolver – a Smith & Wesson – no 61900 fully loaded in six chambers together

with further ammunition on top of a wardrobe in the living room...

At 4pm 21st January 1928, Browne and Dyson were put up for identification respecting the robbery at Eynsham, Oxfordshire, but were not identified, and Dyson was released. The station master, Alfred John May, however, recognised his typewriter at the garage, and also a quantity of tobacco. MEPO 3/1631

When Browne was interviewed, he made a statement admitting knowledge of some of the relevant parts of Essex, that he kept a revolver in his car in case anybody tried to rob him as he drove through the countryside, but denied any involvement with the murder of PC Gutteridge. Dr Lovell identified some of the medical equipment as his property, which proved Browne's connection with the stolen car, but the police still needed direct evidence in relation to the murder.

The police recovered no fewer than four handguns in Browne's possession, two of which were Webleys. When Robert Churchill examined and test-fired one of these, he found that it made exactly the same peculiar mark as was found on the cartridge case in Dr Lovell's car. McBride and Churchill photographed the breech block of this revolver and the cartridge case so that enlarged pictures could demonstrate the match between the two marks (see plate 29). To prove the point beyond doubt, Churchill also tested 50 other Webleys, but no other gun produced the same mark on a cartridge case. Mr Fox, the Chief Examiner of Small Arms at Enfield Small Arms Factory, and two of his staff also examined the weapon and cartridge case and agreed with Robert Churchill. The evidence linking Browne to the murder was complete.

Browne had been accompanied by another man, and the question of arresting the accomplice was then discussed at a Scotland Yard conference, as a result of which James Berrett and Sergeant Harris interviewed an informant in Sheffield and identified a man called Patrick Kennedy as Browne's partner in crime.

Kennedy's arrest was a dramatic affair, which took place at night in a badly-lit street in Liverpool. Sergeant William Mattinson of Liverpool City police approached Kennedy, whom he knew, and was about to arrest him, when Kennedy produced a pistol from his pocket, held it to the officer's ribs and said 'Stand back Bill, or I'll shoot you.' The sergeant heard a click from the gun, but grappled with Kennedy and eventually, with assistance, arrested him. Kennedy had pulled the trigger but Sergeant Mattinson had been saved by the bullet being jammed part way up the gun's barrel because its safety catch was on. Kennedy said, 'I am sorry. I have no grudge against the police but you should be in heaven now, and there was one for me.' Sergeant Mattinson had survived through good fortune and courage, and was awarded the King's Police Medal for his bravery.

Kennedy was now in custody as well as Browne, and made a long statement about that night of crime in Essex:

> We saw the garage at the end of the doctor's house, & we went into the field opposite & sat on some old palings or gates & waited till the lights went out in the doctor's house. It was getting late & must have been after midnight.
>
> After the lights went out Brown [sic] and I went to the garage which is a wood structure & he forced the doors with, I think, a small tyre lever or tool of some kind, which he took with him. The door was opened easily. He first examined the petrol tank & make of car & told me there was plenty of petrol in the tank. He told me it was a Morris Cowley. It ran down on its own weight to the road and we pushed it along about 100 yards in the opposite direction or at right angles to the main road. Brown said, 'We will go to the by ways & escape the main road.' We then went for a long run round country lanes at great pace at different times. We got to several cross roads & corners where it was necessary for us to examine the sign posts, but eventually we got on to a kind of main road on the way to Ongar. When we got some distance upon this road, we saw someone who stood on the bank and flashed his lamp as a signal to stop. We drove on & I then heard a police whistle & told Brown to stop. He did so quite willingly & when the person came up we saw it was a policeman. Brown was driving & I was sitting on his left in the front...
>
> He [PC Gutteridge] said 'Very well, I'll take particulars', put his torch

back in his pocket & pulled out his note book & was in the act of writing when I heard a report quickly followed by another one. I saw the policeman stagger back & fall over by the bank at the hedge. I said to Brown, 'What have you done?' & then saw that he had a large Webley revolver in his hand. He said, 'Get out. Quick.' I immediately got out and went round to the policeman who was lying on his back & Brown came over & said, 'I'll finish the bugger' & I said 'For God's sake don't shoot any more. The man's dying' as he was groaning.

The policeman's eyes were open & Brown addressing him said, 'What are you looking at me like that for?' & stooping down shot him at close range through both eyes. There were only 4 shots fired. Brown then said 'Let's get back into the car.' We had driven close into the bank & backed out a little & drove on in the direction of Ongar. He gave me the revolver & told me to load it while he drove on. I loaded it & in my excitement I dropped an empty shell in the car. The other 3 I threw away into the roads.

MEPO 3/226

Browne and Kennedy were both charged with the murder and sent for trial at the Old Bailey on 23 April 1928. The ballistics evidence was compelling, and both men were convicted on 31 May 1928. The cartridge case proved the vital link between the car and the revolver still in Browne's possession when he was arrested months later.

The *Sunday Dispatch* newspaper of 22 November 1931 later summarized the Browne and Kennedy case with the headline 'Hanged by a microscope', reflecting the fact that microscopic examination of the cartridge cases had provided the crucial evidence to convict Browne and Kennedy of an awful murder. It was the first time that a specific firearm had been proved to have been used in a crime by ballistics evidence alone. In April 1928, a rare note from the retired Commissioner, Sir Edward Henry, to his successor, Brigadier Horwood, summed up the persistence, tenacity and dedication of the investigation:

Dear Horwood,

Allow me, as an old CID official, to heartily congratulate you , and all the officers engaged, on the outcome of the Browne & Kennedy case.

In my judgement, it is the most brilliant achievement of the CID, for at least a generation.

Every link seems to have been rivetted before the chain of proof was submitted to the court, & the officers concerned not only displayed breadth of vision, but exercised meticulous care in searching for evidence in every possible direction. Splendid team work & splendid individual work.

When I next look in at NSY I hope you will permit me to personally congratulate your officers.

Yours sincerely

E R Henry

April 28.   MEPO 3/1631

CHAPTER TEN

Facial reconstruction:
Isabella Ruxton's face is made up on camera

From June 1934, a series of murders took place in which the victims had all been dismembered. Several police forces were faced with the difficult task of identifying body parts, establishing whether there were any links between the cases, and then tracing the murderers.

The first incident began when two baggage trunks were found, one at Brighton station and one at Kings Cross, containing parts of a murder victim. The torso was in the Brighton trunk, and the legs in the King's Cross one. A suspect called Tony Mancini was arrested, and was found to have yet a third trunk with a completely different victim in it. The pathologist Bernard Spilsbury was no stranger to such cases, having made his name in the Crippen case 25 years earlier, but despite his expert evidence, Mancini was acquitted, apparently because of the jury's doubts that he could personally have deposited both the trunk at Brighton and the one at King's Cross station.

A few months later, on 25 January 1935, another extraordinary package was found on railway property, this time on a train at Waterloo station. The police called in Dr James Davidson, the first Director of the Metropolitan Police Laboratory at Hendon, which was due to be officially opened six weeks later. Chief Inspector Donaldson of Scotland Yard reported:

> A cleaner named James Albert Eves ... discovered in a third class compartment, a brown paper parcel pushed well back under the seat.

He conveyed the parcel to the Lost Property Office, and whilst making this journey, he examined the parcel and formed the opinion that it contained human feet... The clerk, Cooper, found that the parcel contained two human legs...

The records of male persons reported missing were carefully scrutinised, and whilst these enquiries were in progress, a development occurred. On the 19th March 1935, the upper portion of a male body, minus the head and forearms, was taken from the Grand Junction canal at Brentford. This discovery was made by three youths, who, whilst playing on the canal bank, observed a sack containing something floating in the canal... Sir Bernard Spilsbury was again called in... There is a strong presumption that the legs and the trunk are from the same body.

Efforts have been made by many persons to connect this case ... with Brighton Trunk Crime No 1, but as far as we can tell, there is no possible connection. It ought to be mentioned, however, that in the Brighton crime, the letters F.O.R.D. were found on a sheet of brown paper which had been wrapped around the torso, and this has caused considerable speculation in view of the fact that Brent<u>ford</u> is the scene of the last discovery.   MEPO 3/1631

The legs found at Waterloo station were linked to the Brentford canal torso, but the case was never solved. There was not even an unsuccessful prosecution of a strong suspect, such as Tony Mancini.

THE RAVINE MURDER AND DR BUCK RUXTON

Then another case hit the headlines in September. Susan Johnson was admiring the view at Gardenholm Linn, a local beauty spot near the town of Moffat in Scotland, when she saw, to her horror, the remains of a human arm in the steep gully below. The police were called, searched the area, and found numerous other body parts, some of them wrapped in cloth or newspaper.

The countryside was hilly moorland, and there would have been very little night traffic on that road. The Dumfries police concluded that the human remains had been brought some distance before being dumped there, and naturally began to speculate whether their case was linked to the others that had occurred over the border in England. The Chief Constable wrote to Scotland Yard:

> The remains have now been examined by expert anatomists engaged by the Crown Office and the following are some details of a statement made to the police by the anatomists as a result of their preliminary examination.
>
> The male remains were very incomplete... The torso, both feet and terminal portions of the fingers of both hands are missing. The female remains were relatively complete and were those of a woman, 30 to 40 years of age, about 5 feet 2 inches in height, of stocky build, dark brown hair, two central incisors of upper jaw (probably projecting or 'buck' teeth) are missing and may have been pulled out after death...
>
> The outstanding feature was that the person or persons responsible for the mutilation had definite anatomical knowledge. In no instance has a limb, head or trunk been separated other than by disarticulation ... [nor] was there any sign of a saw having been used. The mutilator has obviously striven to efface any evidence which would lead to ready identification...
>
> I shall be obliged if you will have an examination made of the records of recent murders followed by mutilation ... and advise me whether there is any similarity between the methods adopted here and those recorded.
>
> MEPO 3/226

This letter from Dumfries was sent while searching was still in progress. A second letter, in October, described how the sides of the narrow gully, about 60 feet deep by the bridge, were covered with bushes and trees. On the night of 17–18 September, the Linn had been in full flood and because one of the body parts had been found a foot above the normal water line, the police were working on the assumption that the bodies had been left there on that night.

As the search progressed, the discovery of a third breast showed that, contrary to the preliminary conclusions, the body that the experts had thought was male was actually female. All the remains, numbering about 70, were badly decomposed, but they were collated at Edinburgh University under the supervision of Dr Gilbert Millar. The remarkable forensic detection work in the case eventually involved a superb multi-discipline team effort which involved Professor Glaister, Sir Sydney Smith (who had returned from Cairo, where he had solved the murder of Sir Lee Stack Pasha using ballistics evidence), and James Couper Brash.

The Dumfries Police believed that the *Sunday Graphic* newspaper of 15 September 1935, in which some of the body parts had been wrapped, was a way of identifying the region from which the bodies had been transported. So a further letter arrived at Scotland Yard, requesting that inquiries be made at the newspaper publisher's offices in London. Detective Inspector Hayward from Scotland Yard then went to see Edwin Morris, the Circulation Manager, who made the following statement:

> I have been shewn two portions of the *Sunday Graphic* for Sunday, September 15th 1935. These particular newspapers were printed in Manchester and comprised the Morecambe Carnival slip edition. The slip edition was of local pictures dealing with the crowning of the Morecambe Carnival Queen, and the copies of this edition, numbering 3,700, were utilised to supply the requirements of our agents at Morecambe and in the immediate vicinity, as per the attached list.
>
> MEPO 3/793

Of the 19 newsagents supplied with that special edition in and around Morecambe, Merritt, the newsagent in Lancaster, took the most copies. Two women in Lancaster, the wife and maid of local general practitioner Dr Buck Ruxton, had been reported missing, so it was to Lancaster that the police turned their attention.

Mrs Jessie Rogerson, the stepmother of the maid, Mary Jane Rogerson, was able positively to identify a blouse in which some of the body parts had been wrapped because it had been mended with a distinctive patch under the arm. One of the heads had been wrapped in a set of child's rompers which a Mrs Holme from Grange-over-Sands had recognized, as it was she who had given it to the Ruxton family when they stayed with her one holiday.

Dr Ruxton came from Bombay. He was a Parsee whose original name, Bukhtyar Rustamji Ratanji Hakim, he had changed to Buck Ruxton. He had qualified as a doctor and, whilst in Edinburgh, had met Isabella Kerr with whom he later had three children. One of her identifying features was her prominent buck teeth. Dr Ruxton was an extremely jealous man, who became violent over the infidelities in which he imagined Isabella to have indulged. At one point, in 1932, Isabella had attempted suicide, and in 1934, she had left Dr Ruxton for a period. Dr Ruxton had once again accused her of an affair when she had gone in the family car to visit her sisters in Blackpool, on Saturday 14 September, the day before the crucial issue of the *Sunday Graphic* newspaper. She was not seen alive again.

Within a day or so of her disappearance, Dr Ruxton had asked Mrs Hampshire, one of his patients, to help him prepare the house for decorators, and she noticed carpets and clothing stained in blood. There had been fires in the yard of the house, and some charred clothing was identified as belonging to Mary Rogerson.

The medical expert team at Edinburgh University found that the left feet of the two bodies exactly fitted the shoes of the missing women, but any positive identification marks, such as operation scars or birthmarks, were completely missing. Some other way of identifying the victims had to be found and they decided to compare photographs of the two missing women with the shape, size and contours of the skulls that had been found. Fortunately, there were two very good studio portrait photographs of Isabella available, taken from different angles. Two pictures of Mary also existed, but they did not have the same degree of detail as the pictures of Isabella. First of all, the skulls from Gardenholm Linn were photographed, using the closest possible angle to correspond with the available photographs of the two women. Then the photographs of the skulls and those of the women were enlarged to life size. Once this had been done, the distinctive features of the skulls and pictures of the faces were traced on to transparent paper, and when these were superimposed the skulls were found to match the characteristics of each woman's face. Further photographic techniques were then used to create positive and negative images, which again showed very consistent results (see plate 30).

The technique of superimposing pictures of the faces on images of the skulls had never been used before but, for the first time, it was accepted by the court as valid evidence. This was not the only evidence, of course: as well as the child's rompers and the newspaper local supplement, fingerprints belonging to Mary Rogerson at Dr Ruxton's house were found to match those found on a hand of one of the bodies in Scotland.

In another pioneering piece of medical detection work, the time of death was calculated to have been around the time of the two women's disappearance. Dr Alexander Mearns demonstrated that the time could be calculated by referring to the stage reached in the life cycle of the *Calliphora* maggots that had infested the remains. In fact the whole case became notable for ground-breaking specialist teamwork by police officers and medical experts.

Buck Ruxton himself maintained that his wife and maid had simply left his home and gone missing, but the evidence against him convinced the jury, and he was sentenced to death at Manchester Assizes in March 1936.

There was considerable sympathy for Dr Ruxton, who was well regarded in Lancaster, but a letter from Bombay revealed that a woman in India was still alive and legally married to him, which might have explained why he had never married Isabella. A large number of people signed a petition asking for clemency for him, but this and his appeal in court were both unsuccessful. The death sentence was duly carried out at Strangeways prison, Manchester, on 12 May 1936. Dr Ruxton used his anatomical knowledge and expertise to conceal his victim's identities; but it was the pioneering techniques of his own medical profession that helped to identify his victims and convict him.

CHAPTER ELEVEN

Dental identification:
Rachel Dobkins' teeth make history

Dental identification can be achieved even if the teeth are not as distinc-tive as Isabella Ruxton's. An article in *Police Review*, as early as 8 July 1904, drew attention to the use of teeth as a good means of identifying habitual criminals, but the solution to that particular problem was already in the capable hands of the Fingerprint Bureau. Earlier than that, in a notorious Victorian murder case committed by Frederick and Marie Manning in August 1849, the murder victim, Patrick O'Connor, a man with a remarkably thin and projecting chin, was identified partly because of his false teeth, rather than the peculiarities of his natural teeth.

The *British Medical Journal* of 10 February 1906 pointed out that medical practitioners all knew that no two sets of teeth were identical when they reported on a dentist's evidence in a Carlisle case. Two colliers, John Torrance and James Miller, had broken into a Co-operative Society store, and one of them had bitten into a piece of cheese during the burglary. A dentist had matched the resulting bite marks with a cast of the suspect's teeth, even though the prisoner had knocked out a tooth stump to try to avoid identi-fication. Both men were later convicted at Cumberland Assizes.

Scotland Yard had been informed in 1933 of a case, in Austria, where a murder victim had been identified by her teeth, but their own first case involving dental identification arose in 1942. This story really began

22 years earlier when, on 5 September 1920, Harry Dobkins (sometimes spelt Dobkin or Dopkin), a carpenter's apron maker from Stepney, married Rachel Dubinsky. The efforts of the Jewish marriage broker who had brought the couple together proved unsuccessful. After only two days of marriage, Harry Dobkins left his new wife because of her continual threats to commit suicide, and got himself a job as a third-class steward on the Cunard liner *Saxonia*. Rachel had become pregnant and, whilst Harry was at sea, she gave birth to a baby boy. Rachel summonsed Harry for desertion, and he was ordered to pay her £1 per week by Old Street Police Court. Many years of mutual recrimination followed, marked by a very patchy record of maintenance payments, which resulted in Harry Dobkins' imprisonment for a short period. There were also occasions when Harry Dobkins had apparently resorted to violence against Rachel.

Things came to a head in April 1941 when Rachel's sister, Miss Polly Dubinski, reported her as missing from home. Polly suspected that Harry Dobkins had somehow done away with his wife after the estranged couple had met for tea the previous day. Divisional Detective Inspector Davis of G Division took charge of police inquiries:

> On 15th April 1941, Miss Dubinski returned to Commercial Street Station and alleged that her sister, Mrs Dopkin, was the victim of foul play, and her husband ... was responsible for her disappearance ...
>
> She also says that about four years ago, Mrs Dopkin was struck on the head by her husband when they met in the street. This caused Mrs Dopkin to have a mental lapse and she was found in St Clement's Hospital, Bow E3, a Mental Hospital.
>
> On ... 16th April, a statement was obtained from Harry Dobkin... On Friday 11th April 1941 Dobkins was walking along Navarino Road ... when he saw his wife Rachel ... he said to her 'Please don't hang around here and cause trouble. My mother is very ill.' His wife replied 'Well, where can I see you?' Dobkins said, 'OK, Meet me in a couple of hours outside the Metropolitan Hospital, Kingsland Road...' They went to a teashop ... and had a cup of tea. Dobkins refused to return to his wife and she said, 'If you don't make peace with me I'll make trouble for you.'

Dobkins says that he knows nothing of his wife's disappearance and thinks she has gone mad...

Eventually ... it was ascertained that between 3pm and 4pm 12.4.41, Mr David Tom Symes ... found Mrs Dopkin's handbag on the floor of the General Post Office at North Street, Guildford... Among the contents is Mrs Dopkin's National Registration Card; her Ration Book; the Rent Book ... two halves of railway tickets, the dates of which have been erased.

If Dobkin's story is true, it can now be assumed that Mrs Dobkin was alive on the morning of 12th April 1941. The only alternative being that she had been murdered and her handbag taken to Guildford and the tickets left in it to hamper any investigation...

I really think she will ultimately be found suffering from loss of memory unless she disappeared to cause trouble for her husband or has become an Air Raid casualty...

Statements have been taken ... including one from Mrs Hilda Nerva ... who purports to be a medium ... she has known Mrs Dopkin for about two years... A séance was arranged and Mrs Nerva purported to go into a trance ... she told Miss Dubinski that she saw Mrs Dopkin in 'country surroundings with water conditions' and she (Mrs Nerva) had a choking sensation.   MEPO 3/2235

Harry Dobkins was employed at that time as a firewatcher in Kennington Lane, London, where a Baptist chapel adjoining the premises had been badly damaged by a bomb blast on 4 October 1940. There had been no actual fire at the chapel until a suspicious blaze occurred in the basement on 15 April 1941, a few days after Rachel had last been seen alive, and 11 days after Harry Dobkins had started his duties there.

Despite the pressures on police in war-torn London, the detectives appear to have followed up some suspicions about the case. They searched part of the chapel and undertook some digging work in part of the bomb-damaged chapel where the ground appeared to have been recently disturbed, but found nothing. The police also took into account the opinion of Doctor Murphy, her panel doctor, who had described Rachel as a borderline mental case. Could the finding of the handbag in Guildford indicate that she had wandered from London and had lost her memory?

However, on 17 July 1942, demolition worker Benjamin Marshall, who had been clearing debris at the Baptist chapel, started to clear the cellar, a separate part of the building from where the police had dug. What happened next was described by Divisional Detective Inspector Hatton of Southwark:

> Whilst shovelling the dirt and rubble from the cellar to the ground level, Marshall noticed a large paving stone lying flat on the floor. He lifted it and stood it on end against the wall and then saw some human remains. The head was attached to the body which was facing upwards... The legs were missing and a substance which appeared to be lime was on and around the body...
>
> With Inspector Keeling I attended and examined them. The forearm, lower leg bones and lower jaw were missing... I thought at the time that the skeleton was that of a very young person who had been killed by bombing, and had it removed to St George's Mortuary. Inspector Keeling, however, ascertained that digging by G Division officers at the chapel had taken place in April 1941, and we then formed the opinion that it was probably the skeleton of the missing woman Dobkin. In consequence of this, I asked the Coroner's Officer to seek the Coroner's authority for the remains to be examined by a pathologist. The Coroner, Mr Hervey Wyatt, agreed and on the following day they were seen by Dr O Keith Simpson who, after making a preliminary examination, stated that he also was of the opinion the skeleton was of a young woman who might have been killed by bombing and that the limbs might have been severed by blast.   MEPO 3/2235

The body found in the chapel could easily have been treated as an old burial, or indeed an air raid victim, but the memory of the G Division officers digging at the site the previous year was the catalyst for a much more careful examination. Inspector Hatton continued his report with an account of how Keith Simpson, the pathologist, examined the body further and found evidence that the head had, at one stage, been cut from the body. He also found a tiny injury that indicated that the woman must have been murdered. The right corner horn of the thyroid cartilage (part of the voice box) was fractured across its base, and was crushed inwards towards the air passage. That particular injury is rare, and in Keith Simpson's experience of more than 11,000 post-mortem examinations carried out over the previous 15 years, he had never seen that injury except in cases of strangulation. The spiritual medium would no doubt have recalled her choking sensation at the séance.

But was the body definitely that of Rachel Dobkins? There were hardly any distinguishing features remaining after so long, and positive identification was therefore a problem.

Rachel's sister Polly told the police that Rachel had suffered from a fibroid tumour in her womb, a diagnosis confirmed by hospital doctors. The womb was the one organ that had remained relatively intact in the body found in the chapel, and Keith Simpson did find a tumour consistent with Rachel Dobkins' hospital examination. He also calculated the dead woman's height as 5 foot 1inch and her age as being between 40 and 50 years, again consistent with Rachel Dobkins, but all these factors were not conclusive. He then used a photograph of Rachel and compared it with an x-ray of the skull, following the technique pioneered in the Buck Ruxton case, and discovered that the skull's facial features matched Rachel Dobkins' (see plate 31).

But the really compelling evidence of identification came from the teeth of the upper jaw. There were three molars on the right side, two of which had been filled. The first molar on the left had also been filled. There were marks from a dental plate and unusual thickening of the bone by the back teeth. Simpson thought that the dental work was almost like a distinctive portrait, and that if the dead woman's dentist could be found, the case would be solved without any doubt whatsoever.

The police asked the family and were then able to find Rachel Dobkins' dentist, Mr Barnett Kopkin of Stoke Newington, a meticulous man who still possessed Rachel's dental records. He remembered his patient well, and, before leaving his surgery to visit Keith Simpson, he drew up a chart showing the work done on the teeth of Rachel Dobkins' upper jaw. He went with Detective Inspector Keeling to Guy's Hospital where, on seeing the skull,

Form No. 1.—100. 19/10/07. *This was the first message to be sent by Wireless*

Sent date

The MARCONI INTERNATIONAL MARINE COMMUNICATION COMPANY, Ltd.
WATERGATE HOUSE, YORK BUILDINGS, ADELPHI, LONDON, W.C.

No. *1*   OFFICE   190

Pref.:   Code   Words

Office of Origin.

Service Instructions *Sent to*

Brookhaven 3.30 pm July 22nd

CHARGES TO PAY.

Marconi Charge ...
Other Line Charge ...
Delivery Charge ...
Total .
Office sent to | Time sent | By whom sent

READ THE CONDITIONS PRINTED ON THE BACK OF THE FORM.

To: *Piers Liverpool*
3 PM GMT Friday 130 miles West Lizard have strong suspicions that Crippen London cellar murderer and accomplice are amongst saloon passengers moustache taken off growing beard accomplice dressed as boy voice manner and build undoubtedly a girl both travelling as Mr and Master Robinson Kendall

PLEASE ASK FOR OFFICIAL RECEIPT.

Name of Ship *Laurentic* . Date of Departure *23 VII 1910* . Where bound *Montreal* . Port of Departure *Liverpool*

Steamship Line,

Names and Descriptions of BRITISH Passengers. *5*

					ENGLISH.				WELSH.				SCOTCH.				IRISH.				BRITISH COLONIAL				
Port of Embarkation	NAMES OF PASSENGERS	CLASS	Profession, Occupation or Calling of Passengers		Adults of 12 yrs. and upward.		Single, or accom- panied by husband or wife.	Children between 1 and 12.	Infants	Adults of 12 yrs. and upward.	Single, or accom- panied by husband or wife.	Children between 1 and 12.	Infants	Adults of 12 yrs. and upward.											Port at which Passengers have contracted to Land.
13293	Mr John Dewhurst	1	first			1																				Montreal
13286	Mr H H Williams	1	"			1																				✓
	Mr. Williams	1	"		1																					✓
13291	Mr Emily F Francis	1	"						1																	✓
7C 14271	Mr F H Whitmore	1	"						1																	✓
	Mrs F H L Whitmore	1	"						1																	✓
	Miss C W Whitmore	×1	"							1																✓
	Mrs Adam, maid	1	"		born				1																	

24 ABOVE The famous telegram sent by Captain Kendall from the *Montrose* alerting the authorities to his suspicions that his passengers included Crippen and Ethel le Neve.

25 BELOW Passenger register for the *Laurentic* on which Detective Chief Inspector Walter Dew left Liverpool, using the false name John Dewhurst to avoid publicity (BT 27/661).

Name of Ship *Megantic* . Date of Arrival 27th Augt 190 . Whence arrived Montreal . Port of Arrival Liverpool
Steamship Line White Star .

Names and Descriptions of BRITISH Passengers.

Port of Embarkation	NAMES OF PASSENGERS. (Passengers holding Contract Tickets as Steerage Passengers should be entered first, and a space left between these and the other Passengers.)	CLASS. (Whether 1st, 2nd, or 3rd.)	Profession, Occupation or Calling of Passengers.	ENGLISH.			WELSH.			SCOTCH.			IRISH.			BRITISH COLONIAL.			Port at which Passengers have been landed
				Accompanied by husband or wife.	Single or unaccompanied by husband or wife.	Children between 1 and 12. Infants.													
Montreal	Brought Forward			1 1 1 3 1						2 2	1					8 9 11 3			
	Thorn Mrs J.C.	1st	Married Woman													1			Liverpool
	Thorn A.H.	"	Nil													1		
	Pattison C.C.	"															1		
	Waller A.S	"	Gentleman	1														
	White Capt M.S.	"	Indian Medl Service															
	White Mrs H.C	"	Married Woman													1		
	Winnett Mrs I	"														1		
	Winnett Miss N	"	Nil													1		
	Gill Edwin	"	Manager	1														
	Greyfers L.A	"	Tourist													1		
	Lelar Miss M	"	Nil									1						1
✕	Dew Walter	"	Inspector of Police	1														
✕	Mitchell Charles	"	Detective	1														
✕	Neue Ethel C	"		1														
	Foster Sarah	"	Wardress	1														

Name of Ship *Megantic* . Date of Arrival 27th Aug 10 19 . Whence arrived Montreal . Port of Arrival Liverpool
Steamship Line White Star .

NAMES AND DESCRIPTIONS OF ALIEN PASSENGERS.

Port of Embarkation	NAMES OF PASSENGERS.	CLASS. (Whether 1st, 2nd or 3rd.)	Profession, Occupation or Calling of Passengers.	ADULTS OF 12 Years and upward.				Children between 1 and 12.		Infants.		NATIONALITY. (Country of which Citizen or Subject.)	Holding Through Ticket to	Port at which Passengers have been landed.
				Accompanied by husband or wife.		Single, or unaccompanied by husband or wife.								
				Males.	Females.	Males.	Females.	Males.	Females.	Males.	Females.			
Montreal	Brown M.K.	1st	Gentleman				1					U.S.A	Liverpool	Liverpool
"	Cadenright C	"		1								Germany	"	"
"	Cadenright Mrs J	"					1					"	"	"
"	Cadenright B	"							1			"	"	"
"	Cadenright R	"						1				"	"	"
"	Reid Carl S	"				1						"	"	"
"	Borden Daisy	"					1					"	"	"
"	Claaton Ernest	"	Insurance	1								American U.S.A	"	"
"	Claaton Mrs B.H.	"	Wife		1							"	"	"
"	Claaton E.H.C	"	Son					1				"	"	"
"	de Cazes Paul	"	Gentleman			1						France	"	"
"	de Palis R.S	"	Banker			1						Switzerland	"	"
"	Emett A.S	"	Europer			1						U.S.A	"	"
"	Hutchinson Ay	"	Physician	1								"	"	"
"	Hutchinson Mrs	"	Married Woman		1							"	"	"
"	Lothmer Fred H	"	Accountant	1								"	"	"
"	Lothmer Mrs M.B.	"	Wife		1							"	"	"
"	Lothmer Miss R.B.	"					1					"	"	"
"	Lyon Mrs S.B.	"					1					"	"	"
"	Dickerman R.S.B	"					1					"	"	"
"	Planche Remi	"	Contractor			1						France	"	"
"	Riepel Felix	"	Cultivator			1						France	"	"
"	Thurnauer G	"	Gentleman	1								U.S.A	"	"
"	Thurnauer Mrs A	"	Wife		1							"	"	"
"	Warren Mrs H.S	"			1							"	"	"
✕	Crippen H.H.	"		? ✕		1							"	"

26 Passenger register for the *Megantic* showing the return voyage from Canada of Crippen, Ethel le Neve, and their escorting officers (BT 26/422).

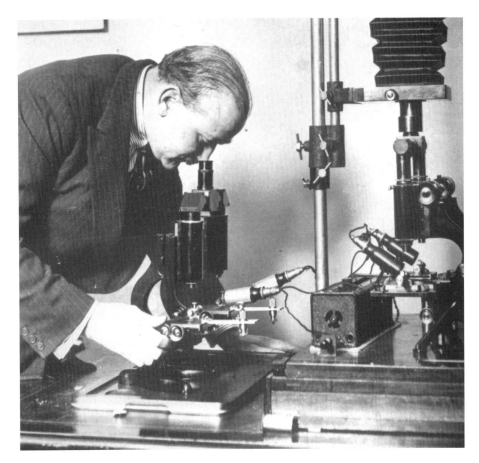

27 ABOVE The famous gun expert Robert Churchill with a comparison microscope designed to compare the minute rifling and scratch marks on bullets.

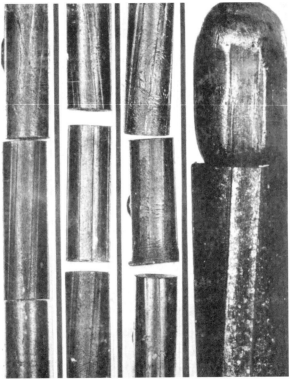

28 LEFT Wax impressions of the inside of gun barrels photographed by Robert Churchill and William McBride to illustrate the variations in rifling grooves of different makes of gun. These were used in evidence in the trial of John Williams for the murder of Inspector Walls.

29 The minute distinctive mark made on cartridges fired by the
gun which killed PC George Gutteridge, and the corresponding
damage to the breech shield of the Webley revolver found in
Frederick Browne's possession (DPP 1/86).

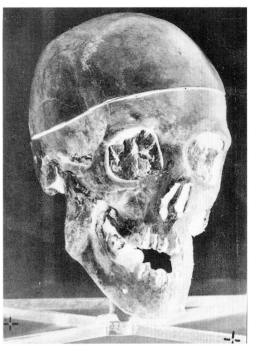

30 The superimposed photographs of Isabella Ruxton's face and skull showing the result of comparing her facial characteristics to those of the skull found in Gardenholm Linn.

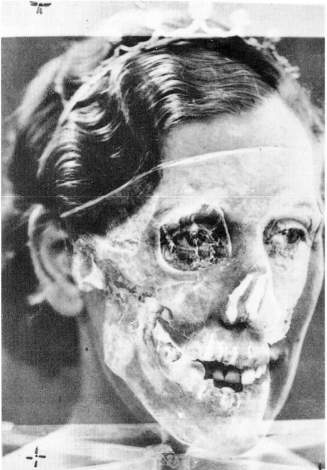

31 RIGHT Photograph of Rachel Dobkin whose teeth were identified by Professor Keith Simpson with the help of her dentist, Barnett Kopkin (MEPO 3/2235).

Photo of Mrs
Dobkin –

handed to D
Keith - Simpson
12 noon 25/7/42
for comparison
etc
K S
25/7

now with
201/42/141

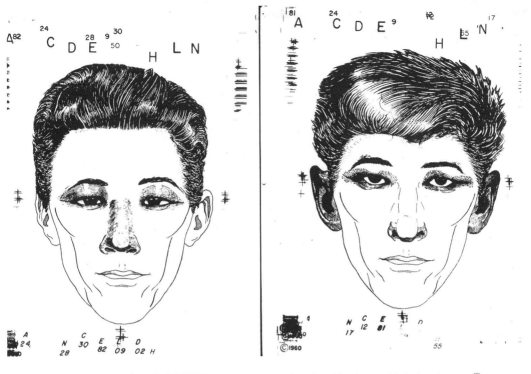

32 ABOVE & LEFT Two *Identikit* images created of the suspect for the Cecil Court murder of Elsie Batten (CRIM 1/3661), and a photograph of the culprit, Edwin Bush.

POLICE APPEAL FOR ASSISTANCE

MURDER

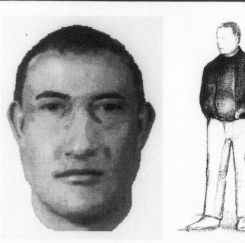

Police investigating a series of murders across London are anxious to trace a man who was seen at Charing Cross Station around 10.30pm on Saturday June 12. He is described as white, 30 - 40 years, heavy build, 6ft plus, with a full/fattish face, short dark hair, dirty/discoloured teeth. He wore a short dark jacket and jeans.

DO YOU KNOW THIS MAN?
HAVE YOU SEEN HIM?
CAN YOU HELP?

Please contact the incident rooms at:-
KENSINGTON POLICE STATION Tel 071·937 7945
ARBOUR SQUARE POLICE STATION Tel 071·488 5212
Or if you prefer contact GALOP on 071·233 0854

AP/52A/93

METROPOLITAN POLICE OR RING CRIMESTOPPERS 0800 555 111

33 Public appeal poster using an *E-FIT* picture of the suspect for the murder of Emmanuel Spiteri which resulted in the killer, Colin Ireland, coming forward to be interviewed by police.

he immediately recognized his own dental handiwork and confirmed the teeth as Rachel Dobkins'.

Not only did his chart match the teeth of the skull, it also contained a record of two queries as to whether Mr Kopkin had fully removed all the remnants of the dental nerves after he had carried out two extractions. When a detailed x-ray of the skull was carried out, these two nerve roots appeared on the film, thus confirming every detail supplied by Mrs Dobkins' impressive dentist.

Harry Dobkins appeared at the coroner's inquest and denied any knowledge about the death of his wife – until he was faced with the dental identification evidence. He was later successfully prosecuted for the murder of Rachel, and was hanged at Wandsworth prison on 27 January 1943.

Keith Simpson had been developing his own photographic techniques at the time, with help from the photographic department of Guy's Hospital, and had undertaken the photographic comparison of the skull with Rachel Dobkins' picture. At the same time, he was anxious not to offend the police photographers who would have been keen to participate in this high profile case, so after the trial, he wrote to Sir Norman Kendal, an Assistant Commissioner at New Scotland Yard, explaining that he had been working on the Dobkins case sporadically. In between work on other cases, he had been taking tissues from the body and having them photographed, or tested, at intervals over a period of several weeks. Having a police photographer on hand for the whole process would have been wasting the photographer's time or could have disturbed Simpson's work schedule.

Simpson's letter recorded his opinion that the Dobkins case was only the third one in history in which such medico-legal reconstruction techniques had been employed, one earlier occasion being that of Isabella Ruxton. The second was an American case many years before when, on 23 November 1849, Dr George Parkman was suspected to have been murdered at a medical college by John White Webster, in whose oven a number of teeth were found. These teeth were examined and identified by Dr Parkman's dentist.

Within five years, Keith Simpson had used the impressions caused by teethmarks to identify an offender rather than a victim. On New Year's Day in 1948, the body of a young woman was found battered to death in a car park adjoining a village hall in Kent. The victim, Mrs Gorringe, had been strangled, and there was a bite mark on her right breast made by someone with distinctive teeth. Police interviewed the victim's husband, who had been seen quarrelling with his wife after a party at the village hall, and Simpson took an impression of Robert Gorringe's teeth; they were found to match the wound inflicted on his wife. Gorringe was tried at Maidstone Assizes and was successfully convicted of murder. The case was more difficult than the one in 1906, in which a bite mark was left on cheese in the Co-operative Society's store, and was a pioneering case where a bite mark on human flesh was identified as belonging to a murder suspect.

Rachel Dobkins' murder became a milestone case, and Keith Simpson went on to become a leading authority on dental identification. The technique has also made a significant contribution to the reliable identification of people killed in air accidents and other disasters.

CHAPTER TWELVE

Identikit: an American invention solves the antique shop murder

Remembering and describing people's faces effectively has always been an important factor in police work. One Scotland Yard officer, Superintendent A. L. Allen, was very interested in the subject, and found inspiration from a farmer who knew all his livestock individually because of small differences in each cow that would go unnoticed by anybody else. Allen wrote a training manual, *Personal Identification,* and encouraged detailed observation and memory for facial characteristics amongst police officers.

He was following the example of Alphonse Bertillon, in Paris, who developed standardized descriptions of facial features into a system known as *portrait parlé.* This led to greater effectiveness amongst police officers in their identification of the physical characteristics of criminals because they had been schooled repeatedly in the practice of describing faces, using a standardized method.

Another man who grappled with facial description problems was Hugh C. MacDonald, the chief of the Civilian Division of the Los Angeles Police Department. In 1940, he was in Europe, investigating cases where criminals had taken advantage of the wartime movement of people, confusion and general pressure on the police in order to perpetrate fraud to escape detection. He found himself sketching descriptions, and then decided to save time by developing a set of different eyes, noses and face shapes, each on transparent plastic sheets, which he could then build up into a complete face, according to information from his witnesses. In due course, he approached the Townsend Company of Santa Ana, California, which collaborated with him in further development and, after a number of years, they produced the system known as *Identikit*. *Identikit* included 525 coded and numbered transparencies, with 102 pairs of eyes, 32 noses, 33 lips, 52 chins and 25 moustaches and beards. Its coding system meant that police forces could pass on details of a description by references to the component parts, rather than transmitting the whole picture. By 1960, a number of police forces had started to use the system.

In London, *Identikit* was first used in a case involving an incident off the Charing Cross Road, London, in Cecil Court, where there was an antique shop owned by Louis Meier and Maria Gray. On 3 March 1961, their shop assistant, 59-year-old Elsie Batten, was found stabbed to death in the shop. Detective Superintendent Pollard, who led the murder investigation, reported the circumstances:

> Louis MEIER, aged 72, an antique dealer … went to his premises in Cecil Court. On arrival he saw there were no drawings hanging outside. The street door was closed, which was normal. He opened it and went in, and saw that the curtain dividing the rear part of the shop was closed more than usual. He pulled it back and saw Mrs BATTEN lying on her back with a dagger handle protruding from her breast…
>
> Dr Keith SIMPSON arrived at 23 Cecil Court at 3.30pm on 3rd March 1961 and carried out an examination of the body at the scene. He extracted the dagger from the breast and neck… He certified the cause of death as shock and haemorrhage from stab wounds of the chest and neck…
>
> Reverting to the scene of the crime, difficulty was experienced in establishing whether or not any property had been stolen from the shop. Mrs BATTEN's handbag and contents appeared to be intact and a box used as a till in the shop was untouched. Superintendent Ray of Finger Print Branch, New Scotland Yard was present, and examined all articles for finger prints.

Immediate enquiries were made in the surrounding area but nothing
was forthcoming to assist the investigation... Enquiries were also made
in an effort to trace an Indian youth and a girl whom Mr MEIER had
spoken of as having been in his shop the day prior to the murder. The
youth had been particularly interested in the daggers at the rear of the
shop and also a dress sword which was for sale...

An appointment was made for Joseph Roberts, a gun dealer ... to be
interviewed at his shop at 53 St Martin's Lane ... together with his son
Paul Joseph Roberts ... the son stated that ... a young Indian whom he
described, entered his shop offering for sale an ivory handled dress
sword. It was wrapped in brown paper ... the Indian wanted £10 for the
sword and young Mr ROBERTS told him to return at 11.15am to see his
father. The Indian left the sword but did not return.   MEPO 2/10436

Raymond Dagg was a detective sergeant at Bow Street who had been trained
on *Identikit*. When Louis Meier told police of his suspicions about the Indian
youth, Dagg realized his opportunity to put the new system to the test. He
became the first British officer to use *Identikit*.

The officer compiled a facial picture of the suspect, first from Louis Meier's
description, and then, completely independently, from Paul Roberts', the
gun dealer's son, who had dealt with the dress sword. The similarity of the
two witnesses' recollections was considered so striking that the *Identikit*
pictures were photographed, side-by-side, circulated to all police stations,
and released to newspapers and TV companies in the hope that the youth
could be identified and traced.

Soon afterwards, PC Arthur Hilton Cole was on patrol in Old Compton Street,
Soho, and saw an Indian youth corresponding to the *Identikit* picture (see plate
32). PC Cole arrested the youth, whose name was Edwin Bush, on suspicion of
murder, and took him and his female companion to Bow Street police station.

Edwin Bush had a copy of the *Identikit* pictures from a newspaper in his
pocket. His shoes were similar to marks left at the scene. He was picked out
at an identification parade by Paul Roberts, but not by Louis Meier, and then
confessed to the murder. The paper in which the sword had been wrapped
had been used to parcel up some goods bought by another customer at

Mr Roberts' gun shop. When police recovered that piece of paper, they treated it with ninhydrin, a chemical that revealed Bush's palmprint on it. Bush had been in trouble before, and had been released from borstal in August 1960. But none of this evidence would have linked Bush to the crime so rapidly had it not been for the *Identikit* picture and PC Cole's sharp observation that led to Bush's arrest. Bush was later convicted, and was executed on 6th July 1961 in Pentonville prison.

It was the first use of *Identikit* by Scotland Yard, and was one of the techniques from other countries that Scotland Yard came to use successfully. The wide publication of *Identikit* images became an important part of some major crime investigations, and a Home Office research study reported in September 1969 that 42 *Identikit* systems were in use in England and Wales. Where an exact match for a feature was not in the kit, some operators used chinagraph pencils to enhance the images, particularly in relation to fashionable hairstyles, and about 2,500–3,000 pictures were produced annually. Some witnesses were not always happy with the line drawings however, and, in an effort to find an improved system, the Home Office backed a research project being developed by Jacques Penry.

Jacques Penry was a facial topographer who was interested in researching links between facial characteristics and character. In 1938, before *Identikit* had been invented, he found that it was possible to build complete faces from interchangeable photographed facial features such as eyes, mouths and so on. He approached the Home Office in 1968 and by April 1970 had devised a kit that police forces could use. The new scheme was called *Photo-FIT.*

In October 1970, James Cameron was killed in Burgh Street, Islington, and the investigation into his murder became notable not only for the first use of *Photo-FIT,* but also the first time that these facial images were broadcast and identified through the *Police 5* TV programme, as explained in Detective Chief Superintendent Wright's report:

> On 14th October 1970 the body of James William CAMERON, a
> Company Director of Beecham's Ltd, was found in the front bedroom of
> his house at 4 Burgh Street, Islington, N1.

Intensive police enquiries were immediately put into action and it soon became apparent, from local enquiries, that it was essential for the investigating team to trace a man who had been seen loitering outside the address on 9th and 10th October 1970. This conclusion was soon confirmed when it was established that the suspect had cashed some of the deceased's cheques at the London Air Terminal and in Glasgow.

On 16th October 1970, details of the murder were publicized through the medium of the television programme *Police 5* with a view to tracing the movements of the deceased on the night of Saturday 10th October 1970. However this programme, local and national press coverage, and intensive Police enquiries failed to produce any concrete lead to the suspect.

One of the main lines of enquiry which evolved during the investigation was to establish, through the medium of the photofit system, as accurate a picture of the suspect as possible. Fortunately a number of witnesses were traced who were able to give a good facial description of the suspect, but, of course, the tracing of these witnesses took considerable time.

Later in the investigation, in consultation with Press department, it was decided that a further, more detailed, programme should be out on television using the most recent picture of the suspect, and for the programme to show the outside of 4 Burgh Street and the interior of the aeroplane on which the suspect was believed to have travelled to Edinburgh.   MEPO 26/44

The process of refining the description of the suspect involved *Identikit*, and, for the first time, the more recent development of *Photo-FIT*. The first TV broadcast of details of the case did not produce any useful leads for the police, so it was important to widen the publicity net to identify the suspect who had been seen loitering outside the murder victim's home. Shaw Taylor, the presenter of *Police 5*, gave advance notice of the picture, and invited viewers to photograph the picture from their TV screens, a publicity initiative that ensured a very wide audience for the programme, which was broadcast on 22 November 1970.

Amongst the many viewers who telephoned in because they thought they recognized the *Photo-FIT* image was one vital witness. He worked as a salesman in a shop in Victoria and had sold an umbrella to a man who had wanted to pay by cheque and had produced a firearms certificate to prove his identity. They had a conversation about their mutual interest in guns before the salesman wrote the firearms certificate number on the back of the cheque, which was subsequently dishonoured. From this information, police were able to identify John Ernest Bennett, and they raided his home in Nottingham. The murder weapon and property stolen from the murder scene were recovered there. Bennett was arrested, found guilty of the murder at the Old Bailey and sentenced to life imprisonment. Bennett had left no clues or fingerprints at the scene of the crime and so it was due to the innovations of *Photo-FIT* and the *Police 5* TV programme that he was caught.

Penry's *Photo-FIT* system was expanded to cater for suspects of different gender and skin appearance. The white male kit alone contained 204 different foreheads and hairstyles, 96 pairs of eyes, 89 noses, 101 mouths and 74 chin and cheek sections. The photograph-based sections improved the resulting images, and the system soon came to replace *Identikit* completely.

The number of cases where *Photo-FIT* was used numbered 980 in 1971, rising in 1973 to 1,259 images, from which 59 successful identifications were completed, a success rate of just under 5%. The availability of standard kits enabled research to be undertaken at Aberdeen University, and this underlined the variation of results that could result from a test sample of people using the kits with a minimum of training to reconstruct their memory of one person's face.

As technology and computer systems developed further, *Photo-FIT* has in turn been replaced by a computerized system known as the Electronic Facial Identification Technique (*E-FIT*). It was developed with a computer graphics company called IO Ltd and launched by the Home Office at a press conference on 4 October 1988. The system was tested by four police forces, where officers constructed 100 faces with the new system and made four arrests during the trial period. There were many suggestions for improving the system, which is now being developed and marketed by a Hertfordshire company, Aspley Ltd. *E-FIT* is in current use with 45 police forces in the United Kingdom.

E-FIT continues to use descriptions given by victims and eye witnesses, and can be programmed almost instantly to create a realistic, facial-composite likeness of a criminal suspect from 11 comprehensive computer databases. Distinguishing features such as scars, glasses, beards, moustaches, age lines, hats and earrings can be added to the picture, and features can be stretched or manipulated on the screen using computer software. The technology must be the servant, rather than the master of the process, and the police have made significant strides in defining best practice to ensure that a witness's memory is not adversely affected by using the computer-generated image too soon in the process. Northumbria police found that *E-FIT* directly helped to secure an arrest in 10% of the cases in which it was used, and other UK police forces have claimed a success rate up to about 40% for the system.

An extension of the system, *Clothe-IT,* was the brain child of Detective Constable David Parker of the Greater Manchester Police. He developed a system for constructing an image of a suspect's clothes, which are often the features remembered most easily by witnesses. Images are increasingly presented in colour.

Scotland Yard started to evaluate an *E-FIT* system in January 1990. Through its use, they were soon able to solve a burglary near St Ann's Road police station in London, when a couple returning home unlocked their front door and were shocked to see a burglar jumping out of their front room window. The new system was put into practice by police operator Peter Bennett, who had to use the computer free-style drawing facility to illustrate the suspect's dreadlocks, as there was no such hairstyle readily available in the system's database at that time. Nevertheless the suspect was arrested.

The earliest major triumph for Scotland Yard's use of *E-FIT* was the case of Colin Ireland, an ex-soldier who carried out a series of five murders, all of gay men, in 1993. In each case, he met his victim in a public house and went with them to their homes, where he took advantage of their fetishes to kill them while they were helpless to resist. The case was also notable for the efforts that Scotland Yard made to gain the trust of the gay community, giving the telephone number of GALOP, the Gay and Lesbian Police Officers' Association, as a contact number. The investigators found that the fifth victim, Emmanuel Spiteri had appeared on CCTV footage from Charing Cross railway station on his way home to his death, accompanied by a large dark-haired man with discoloured teeth. Using *E-FIT,* police compiled a picture of the suspect that was published on handbills and featured on television (see plate 33).

The picture had an unexpected success. On 21 July 1993, Colin Ireland went to a solicitor, admitted that the picture was of him, and then gave himself up to the police. After claiming that he had parted from Emmanuel Spiteri soon after the CCTV pictures had been taken, he changed his story and confessed to the five murders when he was confronted with the fact that his fingerprints matched a mark left at the scene of another of the crimes in the series.

The hunt for Colin Ireland was a milestone in seeking the public's assistance in tracing the serial killer of gay men, and he was convicted as a result of the expert use of technology, crime scene examination, fingerprint analysis, publicity and identification techniques. These have all become routine methods now for Scotland Yard's detectives, a reflection of the fact that a modern murder investigation benefits from the lessons of the many milestones in investigation techniques that have occurred during the history of the Metropolitan Police. The officers involved in trying to catch Daniel Good in 1842, or to solve the Whitechapel Murders in 1888, would have been amazed by the technological innovations that have been introduced to help their modern counterparts. But those pioneers in crime detection, Nicholas Pearce and Richard Tanner, would undoubtedly welcome the support of the most up-to-date technical developments to ensure that the Metropolitan Police fulfils its duty to catch London's modern criminals. The Scotland Yard files will no doubt mark the milestones on the road ahead for many years to come.

Significant dates

1753   Henry Fielding employs special officers at Bow Street

1794   John Toms convicted on evidence of wadding from a flintlock pistol matching a ballad sheet found in his possession

1786   *The Weekly Hue and Cry,* later *Police Gazette*, published by Bow Street

1798   Marine Police formed for River Thames

1805   Bow Street horse patrol introduced

1806   Bow Street foot patrol introduced

1812   Robert Peel becomes Chief Secretary for Ireland until 1818

1821   Disorder at the funeral procession of Queen Caroline leads to an identification parade

1822   Robert Peel becomes Home Secretary

1823   Professor Purkenje in Silesia suggests the first fingerprint classification system

1828   Edition number 1 of *Police Gazette* published by Bow Street

1829   Peel's Metropolitan Police Act. Metropolitan Police commence patrols on 25 September

1831   Italian boy murdered by grave robbers

1834   Professor Alfred Swaine Taylor appointed Professor of Medical Jurisprudence at Guy's hospital
Bow Street officer Goddard investigates a fire in Oare, Wiltshire

Bow Street and Metropolitan Police involved in the investigation of the murder of Mr Richardson in Surrey

1835 Bow Street officer Henry Goddard solves a firearms case by comparing distinctive marks in a set of lead ammunition

1836 Bow Street horse patrol transferred to Metropolitan Police
James Greenacre convicted of murder of Hannah Brown

1837 Sergeant Charles Otway, a Metropolitan Police Officer, assists in the murder investigation of John Brill at Uxbridge
Murders of Eliza Davis and Eliza Grimwood

1839 Bow Street Runners abolished
Murder of Robert Westwood

1840 Lord William Russell and John Templeman murdered

1842 Nicholas Pearce investigates 1841 Eskdaleside murder (March)
Daniel Good murder case (April)
Home Secretary sanctions establishment of Detective Branch (June), which commences officially on 8 August

1845 John Tawell arrested after police use of electronic telegraph to Paddington station alerts officers about his arrival from Slough

1849 Patrick O'Connor, murder victim, identified through his false teeth

1850 Sir Charles Rowan retires as joint Commissioner

1851 Richard Mayne knighted KCB

1855 Superintendent Nicholas Pearce retires

1856 Murder by poisoning of John Cook by Dr William Palmer.
Police Act makes one Commissioner with two Assistant Commissioners

1859 William Herschel uses fingerprints in India

1860 Jonathan Whicher investigates the Road Hill House case
Thomas Richardson convicted on evidence of wadding in his gun

1864 Thomas Briggs is murdered on a train by Franz Müller, who is pursued by ship to America and extradited by Richard Tanner

1865 Constance Kent confesses to murdering her brother

1866 Duddlewick murder case investigated by Richard Tanner

1868 Commissioner Sir Richard Mayne dies in office

1870 Habitual Criminals Register now has space for a photograph

1872   Murder of Harriet Buswell and subsequent arrest of Dr Hessel in controversial identification case

1877   Criminal Investigation Department replaces Detective Branch

1878   Home Office reluctant to forbid police officers from standing alongside suspects in identification parades.
Howard Vincent appointed as Director of Criminal Intelligence

1879   Henry Faulds solves Tokyo burglary case with fingerprints

1880   Alphonse Bertillon invents an identification system in Paris

1881   Brighton train murder of Isaac Gold leads to publication of picture of Percy LeFroy Mapleton in newspaper as a wanted fugitive

1883   Scotland Yard takes over publication of revised *Police Gazette*

1884   Sergeant Cobb prises bullet from a tree to show a link with the murder of his colleague PC Cole, in 1882, by Thomas Orrock

1888 –91   Whitechapel Murders (Jack the Ripper)

1888   Commissioner Sir Charles Warren resigns, succeeded by James Monro

1890   Metropolitan Police headquarters moves to Norman Shaw building on Embankment. Sir Edward Bradford appointed Commissioner

1892   Juan Vucetich solves murder case in Argentina with fingerprints

1894   Troup Committee recommends anthropometry to identify prisoners
Macnaghten compiles his report on Whitechapel Murders suspects

1895   Adolf Beck's first wrongful conviction for fraud
Francis Galton categorizes four types of fingerprint patterns

1900   Edward Henry demonstrates fingerprint classification system to Belper Committee

1901   Preciptin test developed to detect human blood
Fingerprint Bureau introduced by Edward Henry

1902   Harry Jackson convicted of burglary on fingerprint evidence
Bertillon identifies murderer of Joseph Reibel in Paris by fingerprint evidence

1903   Moat House Farm case in Essex features ballistics evidence about the distance from which bullet must have been fired

1904   Adolf Beck's second wrongful conviction for fraud, leading to institution of Court of Criminal Appeal in 1907

1905   Stratton brothers convicted of murder on fingerprint evidence

1906   Torrance and Miller conviction of burglary from a bite mark in cheese

1909   King's Police Medal instituted after the Tottenham Outrage

1910   Dr Crippen murders his wife Cora, alias Belle Elmore

1912   Rifling marks of a revolver demonstrated in evidence by Robert Churchill at the trial of John Williams for shooting Arthur Walls

1924   Sydney Smith compares bullets that kill Sir Lee Stack Pasha in Cairo and identifies weapon from unique marks on bullet and cartridge case

1925   Discovery that blood groups could be determined from other body fluids

1927   Browne and Kennedy convicted of murdering PC Gutteridge on evidence linking a spent cartridge case to a specific firearm

1931   First palmprint evidence given in a criminal court against John Egan

1932   Blood on razor of Maurice Freedman shown to be of same group as his victim Annette Friedson; only 3% of the population has this blood group

1933   Home Office committee recommends regional forensic science laboratories
BBC radio broadcast of appeal for information about Samuel Furnace, wanted for murder
Murder victim in Austria identified by her teeth

1934   Brighton Trunk murders

1935   Isabella Ruxton identified through comparison of photographs of her face and skull
Metropolitan Police forensic science laboratory opens

1938   Jacques Penry conceives idea of building faces through photographs

1940   Hugh MacDonald starts to develop *Identikit*

1941   Rachel Dobkins' murder solved through dental identification

1942   Dashwood and Silverosa convicted on palmprint evidence

1948   Murder of PC Nathaniel Edgar leads to police seeking Donald Thomas 'believed to be able to help them in their inquiries'
Mass public fingerprint elimination exercise identifies Peter

Griffiths as murderer of June Devaney in Blackburn
Teeth marks on victim help convict Robert Gorringe of murder

1950   The film *The Blue Lamp* based on the story of PC Edgar is made, leading to *Dixon of Dock Green* on TV 1955–76

1953   First picture of suspect wanted for murder broadcast on television
Crick and Watson discover structure of DNA

1955   Mass public palmprint elimination exercise identifies Michael Queripel as murderer of Elizabeth Currell at Potters Bar

1961   First use of *Identikit* by Raymond Dagg investigating murder of Elsie Batten

1967   Metropolitan Police headquarters moves to Broadway

1968   Murder of Claire Josephs solved by blood groups and fibre analysis

1970   John Bennett arrested for murder after use of *Photo-FIT* image broadcast on TV programme *Police 5*

1983   Sheffield murder of Laitner family solved by identifying rare blood group of suspect shared by only 1 in 10,000 of population

1984   Dr Alec Jeffreys discovers method of recording DNA data

1986   First use of DNA in criminal case acquits Richard Buckland

1987   Robert Melias convicted of rape on DNA evidence

1988   Colin Pitchfork convicted on DNA evidence that freed Richard Buckland

1990   *E-FIT* introduced to Scotland Yard to replace *Photo-FIT*

1993   Colin Ireland arrested for a series of murders after use of *E-FIT* and enhancement of CCTV pictures

1995   DNA database established

2006   John Humble convicted of hoax partly based on Jack the Ripper letters to 1975–81 West Yorkshire serial murder inquiry

Case notes: further sources

This section gives further documentary sources to supplement those provided by citations in the text. See also the publications listed in the Further Reading.

References in this book are to National Archives documents unless otherwise stated. These are generally available to the public at: The National Archives, Kew, Richmond, Surrey, TW9 4DU, 020 8876 3444. Visit the website for further information at www.nationalarchives.gov.uk.

The department codes in the National Archives document references are:

ASSI   Assize Records

BT   Board of Trade Passenger Lists

C   Chancery

CAB   Cabinet Office

CRIM Central Criminal Court

DPP   Director of Public Prosecutions

HO   Home Office

MEPO Metropolitan Police

PC   Privy Council Office

PCOM Prison Commission and Home Office Prison Department

TS   Treasury Solicitor

ZHC   House of Commons (including some House of Lords)

ZJ   London Gazette

Maurice Freedman

Murder and death sentence: HO 144/16384

Case papers: DPP 2/73

Police Journal, vol. VI, 1933, p. 51

The murder of Claire Josephs

The Proceedings of the Medico-Legal Society, 10 June 1971

Depositions: CRIM 1/4847

Case papers: DPP 2/4484

The murders of Lynda Mann and Dawn Ashworth

The Times, 22 November 1986 and 23 January 1988

Robert Melias

Certificate of conviction at Bristol Crown Court, case no. 872463

The Times, 14 November 1987

CHAPTER 4 Identity parades

Richard Hanney and George Francis

List of persons making depositions: HO 44/9

The Times, 14 August to 15 September 1821

Also PC 1/4194; TS 11/116–17 etc.; HO 44/2–3, 8–11, 48

Mr Richardson

The Times, 28 February, 3 March, 9 April and 1 August 1834

The Coram Street Murder

Murder of Harriet Buswell: MEPO 3/109–115

Attempting to improve the identification process

Practice of placing constables in plain clothes in identification parade:
  HO 45/9356/30237

Identification parades, modus operandi 1922–32: MEPO 2/2064

The case of Adolf Beck

Documents and correspondence 1896–1904: CRIM 8/17

Police reports and statements: MEPO 3/154

Committee of Enquiry: MEPO 3/155

CHAPTER 5 Press and TV appeals

The murder of Isaac Gold

List of criminal cases: HO 144/83/A6404

Daily Telegraph, 30 November 1881

The first radio and television appeals

Murder of Walter Spatchett: MEPO 3/1679

Daily Telegraph, 10 January 1933

Murder of Rene Agnes BrownMEPO 2/9539

Police Review, 9 October 1953

PC Edgar's murder and *The Blue Lamp*

Public Information Officer, introduction and appointment: MEPO 3/2105

Public Information Officer, duties: MEPO 3/2106

'The Blue Lamp', manuscript and correspondence: MEPO 2/8342

'The Blue Lamp', stage script: MEPO 2/9036

Award of the King's Police Medal to Inspector Moody and others: *London Gazette,*
    February 1949, pp. 563–1048 (ZJ 1/1041)

The King's Police Medal

Institution and grounds for award: MEPO 2/1300

Register of cases for consideration: MEPO 22/2

Tottenham Outrage: MEPO 3/194

CHAPTER 6 Counting corpses

Whitechapel Murders: MEPO 3/140–41

Strength and establishment, augmentation for Whitechapel Murders: MEPO 2/227

Whitechapel Murders papers: HO 144/221/A49301A–G

Catherine Eddowes inquest: coroner's inquest (L), 1888, no. 135 (London
    Metropolitan Archives)

Mary Kelly inquest: MJ/SP NE, 1888, box 3, case paper 19 (London Metropolitan
    Archives)

John Humble prosecution: *The Daily Telegraph,* 21–2 March 2006

CHAPTER 7 Fingerprint evidence

Changes of policy in proving prisoner's previous convictions 1875–92: MEPO 2/172

Claims by Dr Henry Faulds to be originator of fingerprint identification 1917–64:
    MEPO 3/2546

Harry Jackson: *The Times,* 15 September 1902, p. 12

General correspondence 1901–09: HO 45/10409/A63109

George Silverosa and Samuel Dashwood

Conviction at Central Criminal Court for murder: HO 144/21617

Case papers: DPP 2/985

Appeal against conviction: DPP 2/1019

Depositions: CRIM 1/1427

Michael Queripel

Depositions: CRIM 1/2650

Case papers: DPP 2/2462

Peter Griffiths

Correspondence and papers: MEPO 3/3009

CHAPTER 8 Ship's radio catches a killer

Gifts offered to 'Black' Museum including letter from Karl Reinisch to
    Crippen: MEPO 2/10996

City of London Police on possible whereabouts of Crippen: MEPO 3/3154

Depositions: CRIM 1/117

Registered papers: PCOM 8/30

Case papers: DPP 1/13

Correspondence with German embassy: application for provisional arrest: FO 244/739

John Tawell

Correspondence and papers: MEPO 3/49

Special Commissions of Enquiry: C 205/16/13

Old Bailey sessions paper: PCOM 1/10

Convicts transportation registers 1810–17: HO 11/2

The Times, 5 February 1814

CHAPTER 9 Ballistics breakthrough

Southampton 'burglary' case investigated by Henry Goddard: *Hampshire Advertiser*
    10 January 1835

Thomas Orrock: HO 144/107/A22643

The Moat Farm murder

Correspondence and papers: MEPO 3/159B

The 'hooded man' case

Correspondence and papers: MEPO 3/226

Also HO 144/1231 (1–24), HO 144/1232 (25–80)

Browne and Kennedy

Case papers: HO 144/10781

Case papers: DPP 1/86

Registers of murders and deaths by violence: MEPO 20/2

King's Police Medal, list of awards 1928–29: HO 45/13418

George Bernard Shaw: *The Daily News and Westminster Gazette*, Tuesday 8 May 1928

CHAPTER 10 Facial reconstruction

The 'Brighton Trunk Murder': MEPO 3/1692

Human remains at Waterloo and Grand Junction canal: MEPO 3/1698

The ravine murder and Dr Buck Ruxton

Case papers: HO144/2067

Case papers: DPP 2/306

See also PCOM 9/796 and ASSI 52/463

CHAPTER 11 Dental identification

Murder of Patrick O'Connor: MEPO 3/54

John Torrance and James Miller

Indictment files: ASSI 51/103

Carlisle Journal, 23 January 1906

Austrian murder victim, lecture on 'Identification by means of teeth':
  MEPO 2/2258

Harry Dobkins

Case papers: HO 144/21852–4

Case papers: DPP 2/1078

Robert Gorringe

Case papers: DPP 2/1699:

Registered papers: PCOM 9/2052

Registered papers: HO 45/22562

CHAPTER 12 *IDENTIKIT*

Identikit equipment: MEPO 13/315

Edwin Bush

Case papers: DPP 2/3256

Depositions: CRIM 1/3661

Use of identikits: a note on facial identification techniques: HO 377/73

Photo-FIT

The Times, 23 April 1970

Criminologist, 1974, vol. 9, no. 31, pp. 19–28

Further reading

Armitage, Gilbert, *The History of the Bow Street Runners* (Wishart, 1932)

Babington, Anthony, *A House in Bow Street: Crime and the Magistracy 1740–1881* (Macdonald, 1969)

Browne, Douglas, *The Rise of Scotland Yard* (Greenwood, 1956)

Browne, G.L. and Stewart, C.G., *Reports of Trials for Murder by Poisoning* (Stevens & Sons, 1883) [John Tawell]

Cherrill, Frederick, *Cherrill of the Yard: The Autobiography of Fred Cherrill* (Harrap, 1954)

Cobb, Belton, *The First Detectives* (Faber and Faber, 1957)

Critchley, T.A., *A History of Police in England and Wales 900–1966* (Constable, 1967)

Cullen, Tom, *Crippen, the Mild Murderer* (Bodley Head, 1977)

Cuthbert, C.R.M., *Science and the Detection of Crime* (Hutchinson, 1958)

Evans, Stewart P. and Skinner, Keith, *The Ultimate Jack the Ripper Sourcebook: An Illustrated Encyclopedia* (Robinson, 2000)

Evans, Stewart P. and Skinner, Keith, *Jack the Ripper: Letters from Hell* (Sutton, 2001)

Evans, Stewart P. and Skinner, Keith, *Jack the Ripper and the Whitechapel Murders* (Public Record Office, 2002)

Farmery, J. Peter, *Police Gallantry: The King's Police Medal* (Periter and Associates 1995)

Fido, Martin, *Murder Guide to London* (Weidenfeld & Nicholson, London, 1986)

Fido, Martin and Skinner, Keith, *The Official Encyclopedia of Scotland Yard* (Virgin Books, 1999)

Gardner, James, *The Trail of the Serpent: The True Story of a Notorious Victorian Murder* [Percy LeFroy Mapleton] (Pomegranate Press, 2004)

Gerhold, Dorian, *Villas and Mansions of Roehampton and Putney Heath* (Wandsworth Historical Society, Paper 9)

Glaister, John and Brash, John Couper, *Medico-Legal Aspects of the Ruxton Case* (Livingstone, 1937)

Goddard, Henry, *Memoirs of a Bow Street Runner* (Museum Press, 1956)

Goodman, Jonathan and Waddell, Bill, *The Black Museum* (Harrap, 1987)

Goodman, Jonathan, *The Crippen File* (Allison & Busby, 1985)

Hastings, Macdonald, *The Other Mr Churchill: A Lifetime of Shooting and Murder* (Harrap, 1963)

Herber, Mark, *Criminal London: A Pictorial History from Medieval Times to 1939* (Phillimore, 2002)

Hibbert, Christopher, *London: The Biography of a City* (Penguin Books, 1977)

Honeycombe, Gordon, *The Murders of the Black Museum 1870–1970* (Hutchinson, 1982)

Howse, Christopher, *How We Saw It: 150 Years of the Daily Telegraph 1855–2005* (Ebury Press, 2004)

Kitchin, D.H., 'Blood Tests: The Four Blood Groups', *Police Journal* vol. VI, 1933

Lambourne, Gerald, *The Fingerprint Story* (Harrap, 1984)

Lane, Brian, *The Encyclopedia of Forensic Science* (Headline, 1992)

Lock, Joan, *Dreadful Deeds and Awful Murders* (Barn Owl Books, 1990)

Mcbride, William, 'Mysteries My Camera Has Solved', *The People's Journal and Angus Herald* (a series of articles commencing 9 February 1935)

Macnaghten, Melville, *Days of My Years* (Arnold, 1914)

Penry, Jacques, *Looking at Faces and Remembering Them* (Elek Books, 1971)

Pereira, Margaret & Cameron, J.M., *The Forensic Aspects of Regina v Payne* (paper presented at the Medico-Legal Society, 10 June 1971)

Price John, *The Metropolitan Police and the Public: The First Five Years* (unpublished manuscript, Metropolitan Police Historical Collection, 1991)

Rawlings, Philip, *Policing: A Short History* (Willan, 2002)

Scott, Sir Harold, *Scotland Yard* (Andre Deutsch, 1954)

Simpson, Professor Keith, *Forty Years of Murder: An Autobiography* (Grafton, 1980)

Smith, Sydney, 'The Identification of Firearms and Projectiles as Illustrated by the Case of the Murder of Sir Lee Stack Pasha', *Police Journal* vol. 1, 1928

Smith, Sir Sydney, *Mostly Murder* (Harrap, 1959)

Stallion, Martin and Wall, David, *The British Police: Police Forces and Chief Officers 1829–2000* (Police History Society, 1999)

Sugden, Philip, *The Complete History of Jack the Ripper* (Robinson,1994)

Taylor, Bernard, *Cruelly Murdered: Constance Kent and the Killing at Road Hill House* (Grafton, 1989)

Uncovered Editions, *The Strange Story of Adolph Beck* (TSO Publishing, 1999)

Vickers, G., *The Bermondsey Murder* (London, 1849)

Waddell, Bill, *The Black Museum* (Little, Brown, 1993)

Wilson, Colin, *Written in Blood: A History of Forensic Detection* (Equation, 1989)

Wise, Sarah, *The Italian Boy: Murder and Grave-Robbery in 1830s London* (Jonathan Cape, 2004)

Index

Acknowledgements

We would like to thank the staff at the National Archives Reading Room for the unfailing efficiency, courtesy and helpfulness with which they bring up so many 'pieces' for the reading desks, and answer the queries of us, the general public. We hope that this book will help to spread the word about what is truly a national treasure.

A number of already busy people have been impressively helpful by making searches in their records, and by supplying us with primary source material for this book. This has invariably been through a commitment to good public relations and on other occasions through the spirit of the Freedom of Information Act. Andrew Brown of the Metropolitan Police Service has been especially helpful in this respect, and we are also pleased to record our gratitude to Chief Inspector Michael Mills of Leicestershire Constabulary, John Porter of the Forensic Science Service, Toby J A Wyatt of Leicester Crown Court, the staff at the Central Criminal Court, Rob Coleman of the Home Office's Direct Communications Unit, Lyn Wilson of Avon and Somerset Police and, from the Metropolitan Police Service, David Capus, Roy Masini and Alan McCormick. Dr Russell Potter supplied details of American newspaper coverage of the Franz Müller case.

Those who work at a number of libraries and archives deserve our thanks, especially the staff of the Parliamentary Archives, Susannah Parry, Ellie Haynes, Kumari Dharmeratnam and Elaine Francis of the Metropolitan

Police library at New Scotland Yard, the British Newspaper Library at Colindale, Julie Ann Gregson of Wandsworth Local History Service at Battersea library, and Maggie Bird, Barbara Street and Effie Gardiner-Armstrong at the Metropolitan Police Historical Collection Store.

Some have been kind enough to share their professional expertise and memory with us, including Margaret Pereira, Peter Bennett of Aspley Ltd, Professor Sir Alec Jeffreys, Joseph Wambaugh, Ken Butler and Maurice Garvie. We would also like to thank Bruce Robinson, Martin Fido, Joan Lock Paul Begg, Michael Fountain, Paul Blenman and Stewart P. Evans.

Putting the book into its final form owes much to the helpful advice, discussions and work undertaken by Jane Crompton, Catherine Bradley and Sheila Knight at the National Archives and we also thank our editor Janet Sacks.

Finally our thanks are due to our agent Robert Smith who has worked harder than he ever expected on our behalf to bring this project to fruition.

PICTURE SOURCES

Plates 2, 3, 5, 9, 17, 18, 19, 24, 32 (photograph), 33: Metropolitan Police

Plates 27, 28: from *The Other Mr Churchill* by Macdonald Hastings (Harrap, 1963)

Plate 7: National Museum of Photography, Film & Television

Plate 11: British Library Newspapers

Plate 30: Evans-Skinner Crime Archive

All other images are from the National Archives.